IT'S
ABOUT
TIME

How to spend your time on things
that are worth your time

BRENTON J. FERRIS

FREILING
PUBLISHING

Published by Freiling Publishing,
a division of Freiling Agency, LLC.

P.O. Box 1264
Warrenton, VA 20188

www.FreilingPublishing.com

PB ISBN: 978-1-956267-64-8
eBook ISBN: 978-1-956267-65-5

Printed in the United States of America

To my amazing wife Danna Jennae. Every breath I breathe with you makes me want to be a better man every second of every minute of every day. Forever will never be long enough for me and every breath with you is a breath of fresh air.

CONTENTS

Prologue   vii

1   Re-Define "success"   1

2   Breathe in, breathe out   19

3   The Dumb tree   33

4   Recovering   43

5   Don't hold your breath   59

6   Truly free   83

7   Enjoy the life   93

About the Author   113

PROLOGUE

They say a book is a captured mind. A book is a complete thought. I love that statement, but I need to argue the validity of the statement with a simple thought. If this book is a complete thought, there is a level of learning that still has yet to be discovered by the author. Having said that, I know I have spent time on this conversation in many ways, sitting on many deathbeds, and hearing the same wish. People get to their deathbeds and wish they had more time. I pray you don't arrive at yours with the same conclusion after reading this book.

It's not an unfair statement to say that people really don't finish things well anymore. We don't go all the way to the end with things these days. This book was written as a manifesto pursuing an existential crisis I see permeating our human condition. In an effort to race to the next best thing, I believe we miss out on the best things. In an effort to climb the social ladder, we miss out on the early rungs of our family ladders. In an effort to take time captive, we end up wasting time more than ever.

But what if you didn't have to waste time? What if you could capture it, and leverage it for your betterment? What if I could encourage you that there are some things more worth your time and energy than others? And what if I could persuade you to think of time in a new way?

I hope this book is refreshing, challenging, engaging, and encouraging. But mostly, I hope you finish the book. I'm not going to sugar coat it one bit; I believe Chapter 7 is the most important chapter of this book. I believe it's worth your time to explore it and to read it, more importantly to finish the chapter. I hope I can convince you that this is worthy of your efforts. I hope I am able to persuade you that this is worthy of your engagement as well. Mostly, I hope I can spur you on to finish what you started with reading this book.

I'm in your corner, and I am rooting for you! I'll see you there.

Chapter 1

RE-DEFINE "SUCCESS"

*"One realizes the full importance of time only when there
is little of it left. Every man's greatest capital asset is his
unexpired years of productive life."*
—Paul W. Litchfield

"Live to the point of tears." *—Albert Camus*

I know it may sound weird and could even be a little insen-
sitive, which is not my intent, but I think about death all
of the time. Now before you go too far down the road on
that statement, hear me out. Or read me out rather. I don't
think about death in the respect that those who struggle
with thoughts of death in a negative way think about it,
and I certainly don't want to alienate a section of those who
are engaged with their mental health by any means. I do
however think about death a lot. Not necessarily the impact
of it, but rather the reality of it. I think about death, it forces
me, even becomes burdensome to me, to pay attention to
how I spend my time. I've been this way since I was sixteen
years old.

The psalmist in Psalm 90:12 wrote, "Teach us to number
our days, that we may gain a heart of wisdom." It turns out,

I'm not the only one who has ever thought about this in this way.

Having said that, I believe that we have a large misunderstanding of how we should spend our time. Primarily, I believe that we spend time on things that don't actually give us a good return on investment of the time. To put it simply, and bluntly, you're wasting your time. There, I said it. You spend too much time on things that should not have as much of it. You spend way too little time on things that should have more of it. This book, in its entirety, is designed to help you spend your time more efficiently and in a better, more fruitful way. I believe it's worth your time to read and hopefully, as you read, it will illuminate areas in your life in which you can focus more of your attention on how much time you spent on that particular area.

Before we go further, I want to be clear. I love a good movie, and a good show. I love music, and I enjoy chilling and hanging out. I love some good leisure activities in my life as well. I believe these are not only healthy things to do, but important. This will not be a writing of all the things you should cut out immediately from your life. As a matter of fact, in Chapter 5 of this book, we'll take a good and honest look at your time and how you spend it, and I'll give applicable options on how you can get more out of it and hopefully enjoy your schedule a bit more. But these options will not be to drop all sorts of entertainment and pleasures in response to discipline. Though, you may have to sacrifice some for the sake of discipline.

I will, however, push back on how you're spending your time and suggest practical ways to spend your time that gives you more return on investment. That return, I hope, is a return of joy, peace, patience, and kindness. Before we do any of that though, I have to make a case for your time, and why it matters. So here we go.

Just Do It

It's a little bit ironic to me that I have sat down to write this maybe 100 times in the last ten years. Each time giving myself an excuse as to why it won't work or why no one will read it. I find myself racking my brain with thought after thought and excuse after excuse until finally, I felt like I *had* to write this. If I didn't write it, I was certain a piece of my soul would die at the feet of mediocrity.

Though there were certainly some factors that pushed me to write this sooner rather than later, one factor haunted me the most: I may not have the time I think I have to write it.

We all do that, don't we? We set our sights on something and then we give ourselves excuses as to why difficult things should remain difficult. As if mountains were not meant to scale, or hills were not meant to be taken. The thing you excused was probably something good for you too. Really good, I'd wager. It was probably something that was life giving. It probably made your heart beat a little faster when you thought of it. It was probably something that attributed to a more complete understanding of who you are and how you engage with the world around you.

From my perspective, this drive or feeling to start something new is in the same vein that New Year Resolutions come from. There is this beautiful and invasive introspective thought paradigm we humans take during the holiday season where we evaluate things. It might be because for the first time all year, we slowed down enough to measure our time, as the psalmist wrote. There's something beautifully optimistic about a new year to get things right. There's something amazingly refreshing about a fresh start, a blank canvas, a potential for infinite possibilities. "New year, new me" we say. Oh, you haven't said that? Yikes!

Then as if by some twisted shift in our thinking, we only address the most basic issues in our lives. This typically involves, but is not limited to, our weight control, our lifestyle, or our situation or circumstance, like this year I want to read more, or run a marathon, or learn to cook, and the list goes on.

So we make moves in our lives, and change some things around. We get dedicated late at night in our beds processing what a version of *better* could look like for us, and boom, out comes our resolution. But not until after this one last Christmas cookie because our diet starts tomorrow, am I right?

But interestingly, our resolve isn't so resolute these days, is it? Statistics show that of all of the new year resolutions made, around 80 percent will fail and lose resolve by February of the new year according to the *US News & World Report*. So, it is safe to say that for 80 percent of us, our resolve is not so resolute.

Then the excuses begin. We go on to say things like, we don't have time, we don't have the resources, no one will believe in us, who will read it, who will care, what will happen if we do… and that list also goes on and on. Our excuses are masked by our attempt to be logical about how we spend our time. We talk ourselves out of good things because they take time from other things that probably aren't as good as the thing we resolved to complete, but we seem to always find time to binge our favorite shows, or watch the three hours plus of [insert sporting events here] on a Saturday or Sunday afternoon or check our email forty-five times a day. Seriously, how many times do you need to check your email? And don't even get me started on social media and the way it's detracting from human interaction even in the home.

Lately, however, I have been haunted, to every sense of the word. I've been losing sleep over the question: what will happen if we don't take the time and spend that time on things that are worth our time?

For example, I have a lot of friends who have given up on things that they need to do because the results did not come quickly enough. I have been in this scenario in my own life from time to time. I believe in the very fiber of my being that to achieve great things we are probably only a mere one or two steps or actions away from accomplishing what we put our minds to. I believe it really is a simple schedule, it's a simple pursuit and a good little bit of discipline. It's possible that ten to thirty minutes a day of focus on that one growth area in our lives would bring us success, over time, but we don't work like this. We want it now. We live in the digital, microwave-culture age where information and the world are literally at our fingertips. I mean, I can order a pizza and it will arrive at my door in less than forty minutes. And I can do all of that from the comfort of my own home without having to take the time to even call and talk to anyone.

To drive my point on incremental steps being a good thing, think about this further. Let's use the example of your weight. If you are overweight and you lost one pound a week for a whole year, you would be fifty-two pounds lighter at the end of the year because, math. Let's be conservative and say fifty pounds total in a year. If your goal is to lose weight and be fifty pounds lighter in a year, then it's a simple break down. Take fifty-two weeks and lose one pound per week. Give yourself some grace on the weeks you lose more than one or don't lose any. Which means you don't have to win the year, you have to win the week. And to win the week, you don't need to stress about the day-to-day, because everyone can process this in one week. Keeping in mind that your weight fluctuates with water and muscle, you may find yourself losing fat and gaining muscle. Even though this would increase the scale number it may also boost the confidence in your body which is probably the main reason or desire to lose the weight to begin with. So it's not the weight number that is your main output, but rather the healthier lifestyle.

When you break it down like that, we would all relish that thought, but then again, it's not based on the reality of sudden and swift results we all have come to crave. Yes, I said crave. This way of thinking takes a goal, begins with the end in mind, and stretches that goal over the course of a whole year. Even if you went for it and lost a half of a pound per week, or one pound per month. How crazy is that to think about? It still gets you closer, incrementally to your goal.

Many of us wish we could find success in such areas; however, without a working definition of success, and an understanding of results analysis of our small increments of work, it sure is hard to understand why it matters. In this scenario, we thought success was a number on the scale, but the success is really a healthier lifestyle as mentioned before.

Then you have the other side of folks in your lives. You have people in your life who start to find success and gain ground, and then, subtly, they begin to settle. They retreat back to preserve the new found status quo because, if we are being really honest, success makes cowards out of us all. Even small successes can become the new normal. We waste time trying to preserve it instead of remembering that we were striving for so much more when we set out.

Here is an example: have you ever worked for or heard of the church or start-up company who got started by "betting the farm" in all that they did, only to find that once they bet the metaphorical farm and won the metaphorical farm enough times they began to buy into the illusion that they actually "own the farm"? This actually drives me crazy when churches do this specifically, because of the high level of theology I'm assuming most pastors have of the understanding that you don't actually own the farm to begin with, but I digress.

Continuing the thought: then you find out that not only do they want to *not* bet the farm, but they don't want the farm to go backwards, so they try to preserve the farm. In their preservation of the metaphorical farm, they actually lose the farm? Interesting, no? I love this analogy because the question that always pops into my mind and has probably popped into yours as well, is this: the farm isn't actually yours. You never owned the farm to begin with, and you still don't own the farm, so why did you settle? Why? It's simply because success makes cowards of us all, of course.

It's an interesting thing to be successful. Success is so subjective to the person who is deemed successful. There are cultural factors to consider, family heritage factors, personal motives, work ethic, drive, determination, grit, and all sorts of differing factors that make up success. Success' definition is derived from a multitude of definitions and it doesn't actually make any sense to hold ourselves to some definitions of success, because we don't view *that* success as successful, nor do we deem *their* success as worthwhile. In other words, if you have to pay the price that "they" paid to find what the world views as successful, then "they" (whoever they are) can have it. So we have to be working with a definition that makes sense to us.

I do believe success is able to be defined. However, by cultural standards, I'm not sure success writing is my forte. Here's what I mean: by all accounts if you look at my life and compare it to the cultural metrics of the success elite, my resume does not measure up much.

My Cultural Success Resume

I'll start with my relationships. I am madly in love with the woman I married. I am married to my lovely, funny, dynamic, and engaging wife named Danna, who is clever, intelligent, and honestly a ton of fun to hang out with. Every one of my best moments in my life have her in the scene. Every single one. Honestly, if you made a movie of our lives it would be full of laughter, hard but good conversations about our relationship, and a commitment to each other that transcends what culture would deem "money making" for the big screen. In other words, our relationship through the eyes of culture is quite boring! She's got beauty for days. Her ability to see me for who I am, and yet at the very same time who I could be is astounding. She is the epitome of grace to me and not just that, also her ability to parent our children with grace and patience is next level. She's simply a rock star. Totally gross, right? Are you even still awake?

But some of you reading know exactly how this feels. There might be one difference, I don't want this to change. Ever. I don't want the culture's definition of a successful marriage because, honestly, the statistics behind their measurement of success isn't promising. And that's me being very nice about it.

I'll take you further in, Danna and I have two beautiful and strong young men that some might know as our children, but because words have the ability to shape or break us, we know them as our mighty warriors. We love them dearly, and if parenting, in the words of John Mark Comer, is "the subtle art of unfolding children", then we are engaged in that reverse origami work every second of our lives right now. Our love is tested, yet unwavering.

My wife and I were, at the time of this book being written, also expecting our third bundle of joy, a little girl. This particular situation ended with premature loss, unfortunately two months before the date she was to be born. I'll go more into that later in this book.

Within that loss, we have experienced a redemptive story through the grace of God as we are actually expecting again. We are expecting another little girl. I am writing this to you now, months after our tragic loss, knowing what is to come in this book about our tragedy and suffering, to say that the God I serve is a provider and comforter.

Now, with all of that in mind, you should know that I work in the Church, and I love it. I am a leader and a pastor and I feel incredibly honored to sit with stories of people who are so interesting in the lives they lead that their stories should be movies.

I firmly believe that God has given me the gift and talent to help usher people into a growing relationship with their Creator in heaven (YHWH or more commonly God) and to be able to try to work the grounds of earth to bring God's Kingdom near. I'm a participant as active as can be in that work. It's challenging, ever-changing, dynamic, and engaging to me. I make a very modest salary that is neither the richest of the rich nor does it allow us to scrape to buy groceries, but there was that one time early in our marriage when we had to. To be fair, it's what culture would consider a decent wage. So, you tell me, am I successful? Well, it depends on how you define the word success, doesn't it?

I don't live the epic tale of the up-and-comer, the new kid on the block, nor do I live this tale of the dramatic highs and lows which we all enjoy the ride on in our favorite video streaming platforms. I am culturally boring. I am likely culturally unsuccessful. And I like it that way. There is very little about me that isn't obscure. I was actually talking to a staff member of mine yesterday who communicated to me that it's really easy to follow my leadership because it's predictable. Shot to the heart? When I was younger maybe.

And yet, here's the rub, I'm never bored. By cultural standards, people might be bored to death watching my life on a television show, because it's filled with so much of the good stuff, there's not a lot of the dramatic pieces in my world to keep the audiences coming back for more. Be honest, how many times do you want to see me round the corner of my street and watch my kids scooter, or run down the road to get a chance to drive home with daddio, really? Cause I can watch that show on repeat all day long and never get bored of it, but it's not a money maker. It would be a cute reel, but may not make it to the big screen for sure.

All of this to say, a definition of success is necessary but it won't fit the definition in the cultural box. I would like to define success for the written reasons of this book because without it, it won't make much sense why I'm so passionate about this topic at hand. Are you ready for it? Here it goes.

I believe success is defined by how much time you spend on things that *really matter*. Stop. Reread that. There are CEOs of companies and even pastors of churches who are not exploring that statement the way it should be explored. And yet, you, reader, re-read that sentence. Success is defined by how much time you spend on the things that *really matter*.

For example, I believe success is and will be measured by what happens when we meet our Creator face to face (read your Bibles people) and give an account for the time we were allotted. To me, what really matters in that regard is my obedience to my Creator. That feels appropriate. So, I will not try to define it any other way. In fact, I'm not sure it should be defined any other way.

Let me take a moment right here and remind you again, I am a pastor. I'm not a political icon, nor an influencer designed to help you understand the spheres of multiple gods in which we should tread lightly so as to not offend anyone. Be offended. I believe there is one God, we can't coexist with many gods because none of the religions trying to coexist agree on who Jesus is. And Jesus pointed to one God, and it is that one God whom you will meet with face to face. I won't apologize for this belief (which is well researched by much smarter men and women than you and me, I might add). In that moment of standing there, I equally do not believe God will look at us and define success by dollar bills, income, house blueprints, vehicles, stock exchange, digital numbers representing our worth, larger incomes, more dollar bills. I believe there will be a different scale for our measurement of success.

And hold up right there, before you think I'm a "don't make money" kind of guy, there is nothing inherently wrong with the list above, unless it's everything you're living for. And if it is, the best way to combat that is to give it away. And while we are on the subject, if you want to give it away, feel free to send me some of it. I promise I'll put your money to good use because you'll never fill the gap with enough stuff to sleep better at night. Instead, I believe that God will measure us on two specific parts of our lives.

I believe God will measure us on how closely and fervently we chased after Him. I also believe that God will measure us on how closely and fervently we chased after people (Something about what Jesus said leads me to this).

For the sake of this book, I will not be doing a large theological introspective as to the workings of God and why I believe God is real and alive and active in this world today. I'd be happy to point you to most pastors or seminaries if you would like to explore that question though at this point, due to the political correctness agenda that seems to be swarming our nation. I'm not sure how many of them would actually answer you without beating around the topic hoping you'd catch it. There are great websites as well to explore God on like www.exploregod.com. Or I'd love to point you to writings by Groetheis, Grudem, Stroebel, and of course the Gospels which are pretty clear in my opinion. I also recently read a book by John Mark Comer that was, without a doubt, astoundingly well done on explaining this topic. His writings continue to be astoundingly deep and apologetic and I'm thankful as a colaborer on this earth with him. Instead, I choose to spend my time on the other part of the conversation that is most valuable for me to spend my time on… *your time.*

COUNTING UP

How many seconds have passed in your life? If I am thirty-three years old. At thirty-three years, unless my mathematics needs some intervention and my calculator on my phone doesn't calculate correctly, there have been 1,037,836,800 seconds in the life of a thirty-three-year-old adult. Yes, that number is in the one billion category. Billion… with a B. This is not including the seconds it's taken you to read this paragraph, or the seconds it has taken me to write it, but it's a general number that is quite large. We sum up our seconds into a number. But what does that number mean?

Let's talk about childhood briefly, what we can remember of it at least. The first sixteen years of my life consists of 503,193,600 seconds, which I lovingly and affectionately can boil down and sum up into a mere sixty-second conversation with an individual. As a matter of fact, I probably only remember about 120 seconds total of my first sixteen years of life. Isn't that intriguing to you? These 120 seconds have led to the retelling of some phenomenal stories, but I really don't remember more than the main parts of the stories that are confined in those seconds.

Also, for all of you younger leaders reading this book, there is hope for you. You actually won't remember most of high school. And though you may not believe it, that's a very good thing.

I only say that because even though there was a large amount of time spent in the first sixteen years of my life, I can remember moments suspended in time and collectively add them up to only about 120 seconds. I'll try to recall some moments.

I remember some of the bigger moments in my life like when my grandfather died. I remember getting into a fight with my neighbors, who were some of my best friends when I was younger. I remember doing a backflip and landing wrong. I remember the tree that fell perfectly between the garage and the house causing no damage to our home and only a little bit to the garage. I remember the house that was completely on fire only five houses away and we all went to help however we could. I wasn't much help in that situation. I remember the house we used to live in and I remember moving. I remember playing catch with my dad, conversations in the front room, watching a storm out of my bedroom window… and the list can go on and on. Yet, when I sum up the whole of my first sixteen years in a conversation, those sixteen years get reduced to one or two sentences that go something like this. I grew up in a great home with parents who loved each other fiercely and my brother and sister and myself with passion. It wasn't perfect but it was fun and we were happy. We didn't have a lot of money, but we got by and all in all, it was a great childhood. Then I got my license and I've been on the move ever since.

It's so funny that we have the capacity to take events in our lives that measured so many years and hours and minutes and seconds, and we reduce them to a couple of sentences specific to the conversation at hand. Then there are the sixteen to eighteen years, the eighteen to twenty-one years, the twenty-one to twenty-five years, and then twenty-five to thirty, thirty to forty, forty to sixty… you get the idea.

So my question is, with all of that time, how did you spend it?

LOSING SLEEP

I'm thirty-four years old currently and I'm losing sleep at night because I feel as if I am running out of time, something I already admitted to in the opening of this chapter. If I'm being honest, it's an incredible feeling to live as if you're running out of time. You get more intentional with the time you have.

Understand this, you and I have an incurable condition that is taking us one step closer to the grave every second we spend on this earth. That condition is called life. And because of the fall of man, life ends one way for everyone. We all have to live it, some people choose to only endure it, or survive it, but you definitely can't shake it. Death comes for us all. Cue the dramatic undertones in the musical score. But with the wave of all that has happened in the world over the last couple of years, I have this underlying question that keeps popping into my brain. Why is everyone living like they can get out alive?

Time runs out on us all! So, why do you spend all of your time wishing you could go back in time to change that one time? When, if you were more intentional you could spend all of your remaining time rewriting time with the time you have left? That one got you, didn't it? If it did, you're my people.

THE TRUTH

I feel like time is running out, because a lot of my friends, and even some of my family, don't know the amazing grace that is in Christ Jesus which is given to us as a stamp in time in the Gospels. I have friends who are not putting their hope in the only hope of the world. Jesus who died, was buried, and rose again, gives us that hope. I'll explain this more in the last chapter.

I have sat on deathbeds and had conversations with people who never once mentioned the use of their time in any other desired outcome outside of "to spend more of it with their families or giving more to God." Translation: when people are old and have little time left, they wish they had more time to enjoy things they should have enjoyed the entire time they already had. Translation of the translation, they feel they wasted their time.

So why waste your time trying to replay a past failure or regret, and fail at making your remaining time worthwhile? Why live your life wishing you would have, instead of moving forward? Why spend your time fighting the current of something that is impossible. You cannot go backwards, only forwards. I'd even argue, you can't move forward, without relieving yourself of what is back there. When you look back and let the past define your present, you find yourself compounding your failure and regret saying things like *I wish I would have.* But when you release your past, unhitch it and let it sit where it sits, you allow yourself to move forward with your focus primarily on your purpose in your future, and not the past. Learn from your past, but don't drag it into your present or future.

We all have things we wish we never would have done. Some of those are a little bit more tangible in their consequences than others, but we all have them. The good news (or Gospel) of Jesus is this: your debt has been paid for those who believe in Him, and you do not have to live in or be defined by your past any longer. In a weird way, your ugly past is a prerequisite for the Gospel to be in full effect.

I believe God has everyone here on this earth for a purpose. Few people spend time trying to search for it. Even so, people search for their purpose in the wrong way. They filter purpose in with bad definitions of success and mix it with what they do for a living as opposed to what they were created to do for their Creator.

I believe that the purpose of man is to give God his breath back, and to pursue others with the love of God to point them back to Jesus. In short, to spend your time, and energy, pursuing God, no matter who you're with or where you are or what you do. If you're good at something and can make some money doing it, that's amazing! But don't define yourself by it. And don't make it greater than the One who created you.

The mission is great, the work is plentiful, the work is difficult and, ironically, time is against us. With that said, let's spend some time together pursuing better ways to fix our view of time and take ownership of it.

Chapter 2

BREATHE IN, BREATHE OUT

"Rumblings are more felt than heard and certainly never seen. They come to you through the soles of your feet into the depth of your soul. Only then do they open the eyes of your heart. They speak of a shift that is about to take place."
—Kembr, *The Perils of Ayden*

Before God created the earth, there was a specific time in history where there was nothing. We don't count this as historical because time, as it were, had not started yet. All of a sudden, something appeared with a word. It's quite difficult for me to see any other option besides an all-powerful God who created everything because the alternatives seem slightly, well, unbelievable. Hypocritical admission, right? I don't blame you for catching that.

Before we get started, I need to make sure you realize something. To prove the existence of God is not the focus nor in the scope of this book. I can account for studied hours from my own life, and for me the existence of God is not a debate. I mean, have you seen a tree? Have you watched a woman grow a baby in her body? Have you watched a woman give birth? Have you stood on the mountains? Have you looked into the stars at night? These things to me are too illuminating and too designed for me to believe any other way, see my hypocritical admission from a paragraph before.

There are many, and I mean a whole lot of individuals who are way smarter than me with a lot of letters behind their names can take this debate into eternity for the rest of us. For me, the fact that God exists is empirical. I'm going to take you to Genesis, which is a script written down over generations declaring the story of creation. I can bore you with my theology on creation at some point in the future, for now, I'm not arguing whether it happened or not, I'm focussing on a specific portion of creation where it seems there is a climax of all of creation. The creation of man. For those readers who aren't quite sure, would you at least be open-minded enough to give it a look?

Here is the account of creation in the book of Genesis:

> *In the beginning God created the heavens and the earth. Now the earth was formless and empty, darkness was over the surface of the deep and the spirit of God was hovering over the waters. (Genesis 1:1-2)*

From here, a rundown of what was created and how it was created begins to ensue. Essentially, it goes in this order: light and dark, day and night, sky and seas, land and vegetation, sun, moon, and stars, fish and birds, livestock, and animals and so on… Then, God does something unprecedented according to the Scripture. Check this out:

> *Then God said, let us make mankind in our image, in our likeness, so that they may rule over the fish in*

the sea, and the birds in the sky, over the livestock
and the wild animals, and over all the creatures that
move along the ground. So God created mankind in
his own image, in the image of God he created them;
male and female he created them.

Why would God do this? Why would God step into time
and create something in his own image? Don't get me
started on the reality that a Triune God created man, and
women, in his own image which alludes to the reality that
we were actually designed for relationships. That's perhaps
another book. But I think that from the very moment Adam
is created, there is this looming reality that we all have to
deal with; to give Adam life after he was formed, God put
his breath into his creation.

Tracking Time

I want to spend some writing space in this book talking
about the breath in your lungs, but it would be a mistake if
I didn't address the creation of time. At the fall of man, for
the first time, time starts because it has a beginning and an
end. These two factors are very important when tracking
something. There's no point in discussing time before the
fall of man, because before the fall of man, there was no
point in keeping track of it. Why, you might ask? Before the
fall of man, there was no ending time frame to the beginning of life for Adam and Eve. There was only light and
dark. So, time starts to be counted when we know there's a
possibility that time will end.

Think of your last countdown you had. Why would you
count down to something if there was never an end date

to that countdown? Why schedule appointments if there's no end? The ending gives validity to the beginning and the ending allows us the opportunity to track the middle.

Breathing

Back to the text. God breathed into man his breath. I'm not talking about the ebbs and flows of his lung capacity as though he was tired. I am talking about the fact that God literally breathed life into Adam. No breath equals no life. So not only is Adam created in the image of God, he now carries with him something that is possibly more valuable and certainly more life-giving than the image of God. He hosts the image of God, which is external and part of our identity. But he carries within his lungs God's breath, which is internal and fleeting. It's precious to us all.

Have you ever thought of the implications this brings for you and for me? I do, all of the time. Fear not, I'll show my work.

From a very young age, I can recall taking account of how I spent my days. I spent my nights processing the days while looking up at the ceiling in my bedroom. Processing how I spent my day. A question I always seemed to reside on in those nights, that would either keep me up or put me fast to slumber pending my answer; was it worth it?

I tell you this because I believe I was asking the wrong question. And I probably lost more sleep than I should have by processing the wrong question. I'm older now, and have much more to ponder at night, but if I came back to that question, then I'd find myself missing out on maybe the more important question. A question you only ponder when you feel like you're older and wiser maybe. I begin to ask myself a similar but much more profound question now, "did I spend my breath well?"

Process this with me. *Was it worth it* can only bring you to one logical conclusion: a yes or no answer that puts you in the conversation of weighing pros and cons of decisions and consequences. Some of those pros and cons may take years to come to fruition. This is a very important piece of information missing when you process this worth-it question, and that's the result or growth areas in which this situation is deemed worth it or not worth it. What was worth it to you at sixteen, might not be worth it to you at thirty-four, so it's kind of subjective. The results come later most of the time with our decisions. As they say, experience is the best teacher, but I've observed it also plays the role of the slowest teacher.

Now, if the consequences were severe enough, pending your grit, you may argue yes or no but they will always be diluted by an external variable. There will always be a bit of an external source weighing in on the discussion. This isn't such a big deal, until you realize that you hold no control over that source. You can't control the consequences in your life much more than you can control the ocean. But you can choose whether you want to jump in or not. In other words, even though you cannot choose the consequences of your time, you can choose how to spend your time. And how you spend your time, will come with consequences on their own; the good, the bad, and the unfortunate.

But isn't it true that this is what gets the majority of our time when we lay in bed or process during the down times? We ask ourselves in our quietest moments, whether or not the consequence, good or bad, was worthy of the action it took to get us there? Even if the action is beneath us and the consequence wasn't severe, we gauge worth based on reactive results as opposed to intentional decisions. We spend the time and energy processing things beyond our control as opposed to focusing on the things that are within our control. That is the point. Focusing on consequences is the wrong way to do it. Focusing on how you spend your breath, now that becomes a conversation about wisdom. And wisdom transcends consequences. If you disagree with that statement, you're still probably asking yourself the wrong question.

With this in mind, I want to ask a better question. This question I started asking myself in my college days, because it mattered a little bit more to me then. The question: did I spend my breath well?

If God breathed into you, you really have only one option to consider. At most, your lungs hold one breath at a time. Their capacity doesn't allow more than a breath. There is no such thing as a multiple breath lung capacity. Some people can certainly hold their breath for longer and their bodies can use that oxygen more efficiently, but the bottom line at the end of the day is this: what comes in, must go out to make room for what comes in again. This means something significant: It means the breath you were carrying in your lungs is a gift every time you receive it. Write that down. You were, and consistently and continuously are, receiving the gift of air in your lungs from a God who could easily take it away or shut off the valve. Whether you believe in God or not, this is true. The gift of breath, like the one you just took, is just that; a gift. And so was that one. And that one.

Drop this into our conversation on how you spend your time before we dive a little deeper into the conversation on breathing and you have got the makings of a very important and albeit different thinking paradigm than most of the culture allows themselves to participate in. If you only get one breath in each moment, how do you spend it? Your breath and your time, as it were, are linked forever. They are meant to be collaborators in the collective whole of your life, ushering you to a life that is meant for fullness of peace, joy, patience, kindness, goodness, love, faithfulness, and self control. But for some, they feel more like adversaries than collaborators. I mean, who wouldn't want these things? Perhaps you need a minute to catch your breath?

Catching your breath

There are few times in my life I've gasped for air. We all remember living through the scenario of the time you were in the pool and you came up to gather air from the surface only to find a flotation device blocking your pathway to that freshness we love so much. We freak out in a small panic attack as if the very air we are searching for isn't already in our lungs currently. You don't freak out? I do. We spend time and extra energy finding ways to get around the object. When we finally capture that air again, we have that small existential moment of what it would feel like to never be able to breathe again. Then we go on our merry way without ever giving it another thought.

Interestingly, there is a lesson to be learned in this moment when you have limited supply. This is the continued account in Genesis that we started at the beginning of this chapter.

God creates Adam from the dust (see Genesis) and breathes his life (air) into Adam for the first time, and if I can take you there for a minute, imagine being on the outskirts of that visual event. God breathes into Adam's lungs and for a minute, I imagine the entirety of creation holds its breath. God is breathing out, and creation is holding its air in, waiting.

The Hebrew words used for this breath are found in two different places within Genesis. The first is in Genesis 1:2, right at the beginning. The Hebrew word used here is *ruakh* (*ruakh Elohim* to be precise) which can be translated as spirit, breath or wind of God. As one author put it, *ruakh* is God in action. Wow!

The breath we are talking about in Adam's lungs, though, is from a different Hebrew word that is slightly more engaging and certainly more active in my understanding. The word, in Hebrew, is *eepoch*, which means to blow. This first breath is not written as *ruakh*, instead, the word for "breathed into" is *eepoch*. Then at the end of Genesis 2:7, scripture says that God breathed life into Adam. The Hebrew phrase *nishmat chayim* are used here. The translation for *nishmat chayim* is literally translated as gasps of life. As author Sarah Fisher puts it:

> So this initial intake of breath is a gasp for air and a beginning of life. Interesting that this first "Breath of Life" starts with a gasp. In Genesis 6:17 and Genesis

7:15, the phrase "Breath of Life" used the term ruakh chayim (Spirit/Breath of Life). Why?

I suggest that the initial gasp is God putting His Spirit within humanity. Once it's there it changes from "Gasp of Life" (nishmat chayim) to "Breath/Spirit of Life" (ruakh chayim). Life, from this point forward, is embedded with the Ruakh (Spirit) of God.

—Sarah Fisher from her blog at
hebrewwordlessons.com

The Spirit gives you life, and it is the Spirit that is attached to that breath. In this same vein, in our last ultrasound I asked about how the baby gets oxygen because I never knew, and there was a professional there, so it felt right to ask. I was told that an infant receives oxygen from the blood of the umbilical cord while in the womb. Sidebar: when I say this to people I get looks from people that very much resemble a "you're an idiot" response. But I never knew, and I blame all of those people for never telling me.

But, at the moment of birth, when fresh air is available there is a flap that closes in the heart and opens to the lungs so that the infant may breathe for the first time. This happens in a split second the moment oxygen is available and it happens automatically. It's not random at all. It's designed. It was explained to us, by our midwife, this is why often babies cry for the first time immediately after they are born, when they engage in breathing gasps of air and filling their lungs for the first time with oxygen, which up to that point has not been used.

I'm not sure I could say it better than this. This is kind of what it is like when you meet Jesus for the first time. Or at least what it should be like.

Back to Genesis. Then the chest cavity of Adam rises and falls with air, and it's either subtle or dramatic, but given the Hebrew word used in this moment, we would probably approach it from the more dramatic side of things. Truthfully, I like the idea of it being a dramatic moment. The air swoops in and he catches his breath for the first time, as if he just reached the surface and had been under that inflatable just a little too long.

Immediately, Adam has to grapple with the reality of being created as if coming out of a coma. The reality of existing where he once did not. Existential crisis? Literally. He breathes and creation breathes with him. All of a sudden, that precious air is surrounding him and he's breathing normally. He's caught his *ruakh*.

If you've never been in a position to become a parent, I want to take you into the delivery room. It makes the most sense to me that this is the perfect moment of creation that God instilled in our walk that graciously points us back toward Him. As mentioned before, the actual science behind this moment is amazing. When my sons were born, the moment between their heart closing and lungs taking oxygen seemed to last forever. First and foremost, my wife absolutely rocked the childbirth thing. She's an all-star so there's really nothing else to be shocked about. But there was this pinnacle moment that I'll never forget as long as I live and it wasn't how awesome my wife was in the moment, I'm sorry Danna.

I'll never forget involuntarily holding my breath when my sons entered the world. They came from a place where there was no external air. They come out of the womb and there is this moment that feels like hours. It's a moment where we really find out if this kid is going to breathe on their own, or not. It's mesmerizing and dramatic. My sons are born and I hold my breath for what feels like an eternity, to watch, listen and breathe. And you wait. Intently interested and invested in the outcome of something that is so natural you take it for granted until you are missing it. You join creation on that day Adam was formed and breathed in too.

Then bursting out of the lungs of those kids comes something that relieves everyone in the room. Our souls leap within us when it happens. Out comes a cry, and in comes that precious air for the first time. And it was only then, that I recall exhaling and breathing in new shared air with the greatest things my wife and I have ever created.

Breathing Deeper

So why do I say all of this? You're probably thinking, we get it, Brent, you need air. Please try to stick with me. It's not just that you need air, it's also that you have to actively receive that air. I believe that most followers of Jesus have missed this lesson. It's not just about the fact that you have it available to you, and yes I've slipped into the metaphorical conversation now. There's access to the air you have desperately been looking for that many people simply don't take in. We don't receive it well. We don't gasp for it. We need to need Jesus like we need to take our first breath or even our next breath and yet most people simply don't breathe in.

Enter into most churches and there is the potential to see this living out in real time any given Sunday morning. I see people collecting air in their lungs and not connecting that air to the Spirit. Not taking in their *ruakh*. They're stagnant, unimpressed, and complacent. They don't receive the joy of life, and life to the fullest, that Jesus offers. Why do I think this, you may wonder? I think this because it doesn't appear that people are even a little bit excited to be there.

Perhaps in our lives we chase things that make us better. Perhaps we chase things we think are the most important things in the world. Perhaps those things are new skills, better cars, bigger homes, more letters at the end of a name, grade point averages, and so on. But one of the most important and gracious gifts you receive every day happens when you breathe into your lungs the air around you and you take it for granted. You're missing out on the best thing in your life. You are so used to it you don't even notice it until it doesn't happen naturally or air is inaccessible. So perhaps, when you finish this chapter, and lay down to rest your head tonight, what won't matter to you is the "better". Perhaps you're thinking the paradigm will shift away from the better, and toward "breathing"?

After all, it's not really about better, it's about breathing. It's about taking in air and connecting that to your Father in heaven. How did you spend your breath today? Every incoming square inch of air in your lungs, how did that get spent? The gift that you took for granted, and didn't have to worry about where it was coming from, how did it go?

It affects every area of our lives. From efforts, to energy, to words we say, to the things we did when we weren't even thinking about air. How did you spend that air you were graciously given? What did you chase today that made you more connected to breathing? What did you chase today that made you feel more connected to God? Would you be content at night if you had spent your air in your lungs better than you did? I believe you would.

Try it. Put this chapter down, focus on the air in your lungs, and process what it would be like to view that air as a gift from God. As spoken word and hip hop artist Propaganda would say, "Give God his breath back, you owe him."

Well, now you know. The air in your lungs is a tangible and fleeting gift. So, answer this question, dear reader, how are you going to spend it?

Chapter 3

THE DUMB TREE

*"I don't presume to tell you what to do with your past,
but know there are some of us who care about
what you do with your future."*
—Alfred, from Batman Begins

When I was handed the keys to my very first car, my dad gave me a list of three very simple rules to follow.

Rule 1: Have fun. What a great dad! He told me to get out there and go for it! The world was waiting and my stallion only needed to be fueled up and occasionally have an equivalent of a blood transfusion every 3000-5000 miles. My stallion at the time was a 1997 Jeep Wrangler that was teal in color and only boasted four cylinders of power. And I have to say, it was one of the best cars I've ever driven.

It was an amazing moment for my father to release me into the world. I felt truly released for the first time in my life. It felt like a rush of freedom mixed with a sense of adventure and a dash of responsibility. I was on my way. In later chapters, I'll explain why this is so important in the world. I'm not sure if he knew what he was doing, or if he knew *exactly* what he was doing, but ever since that day, I have been on the go.

Before I continue, I feel compelled to put this little secret of wisdom into this writing. When you reach a certain age, there are no rules. You can do whatever you want. The reason I say this is I work with young people. They look at me at twenty-one and tell me of their plight. They say things like "I work at this dead-end job and have nothing to show for it". And I tell them that they are twenty-one and have a lot of time to go for it. I let them in on the secret people don't share, that there are no rules and they light up. Almost as if they don't believe me. Truthfully, it's dangerous to tell you this, because you might read it and believe it. You might dare to dream of better ways to spend your time and energy and breath in this world. You may actually do something that you love with that breath. I hope it's something that helps people. There are no rules. There is only accountability in how you spend your time and breath. All it takes to make it in this life is time, air, and a little bit of money.

You can move anywhere you want, learn anything you want, decide anything you want. You grow up being told that there are a bunch of rules you need to follow. But there are none. Get out there. Shake things up. Spend your time and breath on the things you love and that are worth it. Consider this your permission to have a rule-1 release to have fun with the breath God gave you. But know that you'll be responsible and accountable for what you spent it on, so spend wisely because connected to the reality that there are no rules, is the equal and parallel reality that there is a better *way* to live your life. More on that in the coming chapters. Chapter 5 in particular is a practical doozy.

Rule 2: This rule was simple enough. My dad asked me while I was on my adventures and doing all of the things, that I would refrain from driving between 1:30 AM to 3:30 AM (Eastern time zone, if you must know). No matter where I was on the road at that time, I would either choose to stay where I was at, sleep in my car, pull over and get off of the road. My dad realized very quickly in his life that the only thing worse than releasing me on the world to live my adventures, was to wake up to a call in the middle of the night to hear about an accident I had been involved in where someone was driving impaired and I was the consequence of that decision. So, he asked me not to drive between those times. And I listened. When I say I listened, I mean I really listened. I slept in my Jeep in a lot of church parking lots, and at truck stops and all sorts of fun places.

Why did I do that? Because the why of the rule made sense to me. Until I was the age of twenty or twenty-one, I never drove between the hours of 1:30 to 3:30 AM. Weird, right? I thought I should insert a tangent paragraph about why listening to your dad, who gives you the freedom to choose your own curfew until you mess it up, is a great thing to do to gain more freedom and trust from your father. That may be for a different time.

Rule 3: This rule was a bit vague if you ask me. My father asked me, as a testament of will, to follow another simple rule. My dad asked me to not be dumb. Super vague and wide open. No description on this one. A simple don't be dumb. Felt simple enough, I mean, how hard could it be?

Now, to a sixteen-year-old, this is a vague rule. But to an eighteen-year-old in college, this is even more vague.

Continuing into the years, this rule gets more complicated and yet more simplified in a weird way. Don't be dumb. Got it. Thanks, Dad. Wait... what does that mean again? How will I know? Where is the dumb line? Where is the dumb tree that I need to stay away from? Will it be marked so I can see it? Or is it like a pit that you fall into?

For the most part, I followed that last rule. But inevitably, as time, luck, and circumstance would have it, I would find myself getting dangerously close to the dumb tree, and spend a majority of my time looking at the dumb tree without climbing it. And wouldn't you know it, as fate would have it, again, eventually I would climb the dumb tree, and go all the way to the top. I would break rule number three!

Please don't tell my dad this. I respect him way too much for him to think of me in any other way than perfect (I can hear the actual parents laughing because they know more than anyone their kids aren't perfect). I know I'm not alone. I'm certain you've climbed the dumb tree a time or two in your life. Be honest, you know you have. If you don't think you have, let me explain why I think you have.

The dumb tree is the metaphor for the decision you made to get you into a certain amount of circumstances that yielded a particular amount of consequences. It's actually most likely the thing you spend most of your time regretting, wishing you never, trying to rewrite, change, go back, or make amends for... etc. Sometimes you even get embarrassed about the good dumb stuff you did that wasn't a big deal, but still mattered. These are the stories you tell people with a hint of shame and a couple laughs the older you get.

Always ending with some sort of sentiment statement like "I was so dumb".

The dumb tree is not a physically real tree (unless it is for you), but it's a tree you've climbed. And quite honestly, some people are still up there. Some of *you* may still be up there. The people usually driving on the highway around me at any given time are definitely still up there for various reasons.

However, it is true, I've climbed this tree. Some of you reading this book have climbed this tree. As Troy Bolton, from *High School Musical* would attest, we are all in this together. As unfortunate as this is, here is the rub, no one is exempt.

No one is sacred. No one is set apart on this one. Everyone has been up that tree. The dumb tree represents a lot of things to a lot of people. Some of us only climbed the dumb tree once or twice, learned our lesson, and got out of there. Some of us climbed that thing over and over and over again, and built a fort in it, fell out of it, climbed back into it, and so on and so forth. Don't believe me? Have you ever heard of addiction being something that someone fell into? They climbed the tree one day and never came down? No, it's something that we put our time and energy into. It's an active choice on how we spend our breath.

And still, others, you know them personally, you can insert their name if you'd like, maybe it is even you. Others want to live in the tree it seems like. They want to start a whole community in the tree. They seem to never want to come out of the tree and we sit here and wonder ourselves if they'll ever come down out of the dumb tree, and it's not looking promising. And when they tell you their stories (because it would never be you up there), we see the red flags and the warning signs and we honestly just don't care enough to tell them that they're being dumb. We think if it doesn't affect us, it doesn't matter. I have a friend or two who live up there to this day. They know how I feel, don't worry.

The funny part about the dumb tree is that we think it offers us a better perspective, maybe more freedom, maybe even a better life or outcome, but the reality is the dumb tree only wastes our time, and fills our time with us wishing we hadn't wasted our time up there in the first place. It takes your breath and sends it in the wrong direction. Instead of giving God his breath back, you waste it by spending it to give your past its breath back.

It's not just the time in the tree that we spend, but it's also recalling our time back to the dumb tree every time we have a "wish I would have never" moment. You spend countless seconds wondering how you got into the dumb tree financially, sexually, physically, relationally, spiritually, and metaphorically. But as we continue our conversation about your time, it feels not only important, but urgent for me to alleviate some of those seconds for you. Check out this study about brain development among young people.

> It doesn't matter how smart teens are or how well they scored on the SAT or ACT. Good judgment isn't something they can excel in, at least not yet.

> The rational part of a teen's brain isn't fully developed and won't be until age 25 or so. In fact, recent

research has found that adult and teen brains work differently. Adults think with the prefrontal cortex, the brain's rational part. This is the part of the brain that responds to situations with good judgment and an awareness of long-term consequences. Teens process information with the amygdala. This is the emotional part. In teen's brains, the connections between the emotional part of the brain and the decision-making center are still developing—and not always at the same rate. That's why when teens have overwhelming emotional input, they can't explain later what they were thinking. They weren't thinking as much as they were feeling.

—University of Rochester Medical Center Study

Take another look at that second statement in the first paragraph. It's not something you *can* excel at, at least not yet. What? You mean I was not even able to excel at this even if I tried?

So there you have it. You're off the hook for everything before the median age of twenty-five. You actually didn't know any better. In other words, you were dumb! And if you're past the twenty-five years of age mark and making dumb decisions, you're probably not seeing the consequences of your decisions and how they are affecting those around you. Especially those you love.

So, why don't you come on down from the dumb tree and we'll get to work on what really matters. What really matters is how you spend your time and how you give back that air in your lungs to something greater than you have been.

The dumb tree is a prison. It keeps you wishing you had or hadn't done things in your past, that pushes you to not do things in your present. Ultimately, it steals what you will do in the future. It's taken us two chapters to get here, but this is what this book is all about. You should be doing more in your present, and worrying far less about your past and future.

Your present will become your past in your future, so let's make sure we make the most of it so you don't have to keep replaying it and wasting time on it. There's so much to pursue that is more worthy of your time than the time you spend self-loathing the past. And it will only waste more time in your life if you continue to live in the past as we've communicated in the previous two chapters. There are two things you have going for you that are more precious than any other thing in the world. The two are the breath in your lungs, and the time you have left to fill your lungs deeply with the good stuff.

Our past makes prisoners of us all if we let it. It's time to break free from the chains we put ourselves in. Get out of the dumb tree, and walk toward something more, something greater. A version of you that was created for more than a season of stupidity or ignorance. A version of yourself who has a future out there. Even a version of yourself who is forgiven and forgives for a season of decisions that you cannot control any longer. You'll be so glad you did. And remember, the only person keeping you in the tree is you. So come on out, get down, and let's work through why you stayed up there for so long, or why you keep going back up there.

The rest of the world is waiting for you to join us down here, as far away from the dumb tree as possible. Why not give it a try?

Chapter 4

RECOVERING

"Before my father died, he said the worst thing about growing old was that other men stopped seeing you as dangerous. I've always remembered that, how being dangerous was sacred; a badge of honor. You live your life by a code, an ethos. Every man does. It's your shoreline. It's what guides you home. And trust me, you're always trying to get home."
—Lt. Rorke, Act of Valor

There is a lot more to be said about the connection between breathing and your time, but I think you're picking up what I'm laying down. I feel as though I may have covered a lot of it in the chapters above. I can go on and on and on. Particularly when we talk in Chapter 3 about not wasting your time on your past, there is one particular season of life in which the time you spend is important and not a waste, depending on how you go about it. That particular season of our lives when it is worth our time to go through slowly is the moment when we have suffered loss.

November 6

In November of 2021, my wife and I suffered from the loss of our baby girl after only twenty-seven weeks of pregnancy. The story, though some parts are not to be read or known, is important. It is incredibly close to my feelings, and is hard to discuss. The story matters by way of how to work through these moments without wasting your time or breath.

I'm not an expert by any means, but I'll tell you how I experienced it and how my counselor and friends have helped me through the most difficult season I have had to walk through to date. Keep in mind, we were surrounded by people who shared a similar belief in Jesus. I truly don't know how people engage in suffering without the hope of Jesus honestly.

I wrote this chapter one month after our loss so it would be fresh. You'll notice some edits that have more hindsight, but I wanted to share our story as raw as I could.

It was an incredibly draining week and a half of life. If you're a parent, you're already lacking sleep in general, but that week both of our children were not resting well. We were up multiple times in the night.

If you are from Michigan, we have five seasons of the year. First we have the fall. There is nothing like a Michigan fall day. It's amazing, truly. Then fall turns into winter, which I am convinced no one really loves, but we all like wintery things, so we deal with it. Plus there seems to be a survival mentality to winter that makes Michiganders tougher and nicer in general, especially when the sun is out. Then that makes way for spring. Nestled in those three seasons is a fourth season, which we endearingly call flu-season. It comes and goes, pandemic aside, it's a season of full-on runny noses, and coughs and allergies even, which also are not ideal. Following all of those, is our season of construction, I mean summer. Which is the best, especially after you've survived winter. Why do I tell you this? If you're a parent, and your kids like to play outside, it's inevitable you won't sleep much sometimes.

So, there we were, in an already draining week and a half of life. Kids up and down at night, tossing and turning and all of the in-between. It was around midnight, my wife couldn't feel our daughter, Lennon Mae, moving. She called the midwives and they tried some things. At 3 AM, it was clear she needed to head in to the hospital to get a closer look at things. In hindsight, my wife knew, for a couple of reasons, that this wasn't going to end well. At 4 AM, I received the worst news I've ever received. A simple text message, from my wife that read "she's gone".

I can't fully describe all of the feelings I had in that moment. I can't even explain how they hit me all at once, but they did. Intense, devastating emotions hit me harder than any other moment in my life. Not only that, but after being physically and emotionally drained from a week of hard parenting and loving our two sons through their ailments, we now were walking through what I confidently can say was the worst day of our lives at the writing of this book.

Our baby girl was gone, and so I sat, crying, at 4 AM in my living room for an hour, praying to God asking him for comfort, wisdom, discernment, courage, and strength.

When I arrived at the hospital, Danna and I sat together and cried. We shared every feeling we were feeling. The nursing staff, midwives, and doctors were all amazing, and they engaged with us and stepped into the pain with us in a way that was so beautiful our burden truly felt carried by them to some degree throughout the day. Some even requested our case when they got on shift and ran toward us. And we sat, crying together. We measured every breath we were taking, and this day, unlike the births of my sons, I found myself holding my breath for a different reason. The day would continue to have ups and downs as my wife was actually not out of the woods of danger yet. By the time we had her squared away, and returned home that evening around midnight, after the worst twenty-four hours of our lives, we had nothing but to hold each other, cry, and pray.

The hardest days of our lives are the most defining days of our lives. There are no words to express the sorrow and anguish we have felt in the loss of our daughter. There is no way to describe to you in words or even emotions how empty a void can be and how deep a wound can go. But there is something about living through your worst day that develops a rare optimism in you. You almost feel guilty for having it. It gives you confidence in a way as if surviving your worst day is a tip of the hat from life saying you're going to be okay, even though in *that* moment you know you're far from okay.

While in the hospital, around 4:00 PM, I looked at my wife and said the following:

"You know what is interesting about knowing you are living through your worst day of your life?"

"What's that?" She replied with tears in her eyes.

"We know we can live through it."

You're sitting there reading this, saying something like *oh, come on, no you did not say that.* Yes, yes I did. And I really cannot take credit for the thought, because it felt like a thought that came to me. In our worst moments of our shared life together, our Savior and Comforter was near us, and consoling us in a real way with perspective, community, and encouragement.

Eventually we would leave the hospital without more than a story to show for our worst day. Twenty-four hours summed up into one heading; that is 86,400 seconds. I'll never forget the weight of my child in my arms as she lay there unable to form breath in her lungs. Unable to *eepoch* and violently gasp for air like she was meant to. I'll never forget kissing her goodbye, a gift most fathers do not get the luxury of. I held her there, as she was unable to gasp for life. Unable to fill her lungs with air. And I wept quietly, and held my breath, hoping for some other alternative outcome that would never come, praying for some other option.

Why would I say all of this? What's the point of this story? The point of this story is the reality that while you suffer, it is not a waste of time. It can only be a waste of time if you stay in your suffering. If you choose to wallow in your suffering, as opposed to stepping into and out of it, and allowing the pain to be painful. So many people suffer quietly, and yet, we were not designed to do this. At creation, we were created by a triune God, which means we were created for relationship, remember? We were relationally created in God's own image, and our relationships matter.

Many people do not want to step toward the pain, because the pain is well, painful. They don't want to get over the pain of their worst days because pain can be an unhealthy companion and connection to the ones we lost, but a companion to them nonetheless. We think it links us to them, but it really causes us to suffer more and it wastes the air we breathe. I believe that people need to run toward the pain, because on the other side of that pain is something better and more complete. On the other side of that pain is a realization that your worst days can lead you to your best days because it is our worst days that allow us to breathe better breaths.

I can't tell you why your worst day happened to you. I cannot in good conscience tell you to forget about it and move on quickly either. I know a part of me will never forget what that room was like, or the weight of Lennon Mae.

I can however tell you that we all end up with no more time, no more breath. Eventually, our breath runs out for us all. As a matter of fact, this is not an original thought, the writer in Ecclesiastes writes, "It is better to be a funeral, than a wedding, because we all end up there." This is my version of course, but the thought is the same.

The actual scripture, in the NIV is this:

> *"it is better to go to a house of mourning than to go to a house of feasting, for death is the destiny of everyone; the living should take this to heart."*
> (Ecclesiastes 7:2)

You catch that? No one makes it out alive. Eventually we all end up with no time, and no air, so what did we do with it? I realize our situation is different from yours. And to suffer is important, to grieve is healthy. It's okay to not be okay, but it is not okay to stay there. Take this to heart as you spend your time in your hurts and griefs. It should, at some point to some degree, fuel you to live. So as you suffer, and grieve, allow me, if you would, to sit beside you and encourage you by trying to help you understand the best way to do it, so you do not waste your time.

Living

I think one of the main reasons I am so passionate about this is that the "living" don't often look very alive in my observation.

We talk about being fully alive, a gift that only Jesus can bring to you really, but the majority of the people I see walking around and breathing air aren't alive. They're zombies in a state of dormancy. They're hollow shells, ghosts of the truest versions of themselves. Before we go further, I'm not promoting a "be true to yourself" theology, because since when have men been true to themselves and it's been better for everyone? Go ahead, I'll wait for the answer. I *am* however promoting a real understanding of what it means to be living. And to do that, some of you need to recover from what it is that holds you back from really living your life to the fullest sense of the word.

There are a few ways in which you can move into the next steps of recovery if you suffer and grieve and really if you're anxious or depressed as well. Because I am not an expert on the situation and I highly recommend anyone reading this book to seek professional counseling and medical help if you are suffering from loss or grief. I have however, as a pastor, sat in many different rooms and houses of mourning.

I've been there with people in situations like ours. I've sat in the room when the senior in high school overdosed, or the young man shot himself with a shotgun and ended his life before it began. I've sat in rooms of suffering, hurt, pain, and frustration. I've sat in the room with the suicidal thoughts. All of these things are tragic and traumatic in their own way.

I also sat on the deathbed of the elderly. One particular situation changed me forever and is likely the main argument for the need of this book to be written. As I sat there on the deathbed, with the woman who would teach me the most valuable lesson of my life, I asked her questions upon questions upon questions. Though one time she answered unprompted. This unprompted response was the key to my understanding of time.

"I don't wish I worked more. I wish I spent more time living more."

I was blown away. So would you have been. Her time drawing to an end, getting more and more precious every second, and she saw it fit to take the time to persuade me to live more.

Why all of this? Because I believe you need to recover from your paradigm that says time is eternal and everlasting. And if you do that, I believe you will be able to recover better from your ailments. To help the process, though, allow me to give you some practical advice to walk away with from this chapter.

Recovering

I believe in counseling. Our story is our story, but yours is yours. Many have lost and grieved in different ways. Many experience this life in different ways. It's not the same for everyone, which I think is beautiful in its own way, but I believe it's incredibly necessary to grieve and talk, and can be done well.

However, before I begin to try to encourage you to walk through some recovery elements, know that I am incredibly sorry for the loss you've experienced in your life. I don't need to know you personally to know how loss can impact people. It hurts. It sucks. I know this by way of experience, and that is heartbreaking. And loss is tragic and traumatic. There is no other way to describe it.

But may I offer an alternative mentality paradigm to your situation, if I could be so bold? As tragic as these moments are, they can also be quite beautiful, can they not? To know that you're able to live through the worst days, to be able to look toward the best days? To be in tune with the air in your lungs and the time you are given. To *live* and *know* that you are living to the fullest you can? To be able to look around you and know that every experience in your life is worthy of your full attention?

Think back to the times you're most in touch with your breathing? They're the times you feel as though you cannot breathe. Under a raft for example in the pool. They connect us to something bigger, something better, something more human and mortal. It persuades us that maybe, just maybe our time, our breath, our air is a gift, and not a curse.

I want you to heal from your wounds, more than I can explain in one chapter. I'd take them from you if I could, to allow you to be free from the chains and tyranny of pain. But I don't want you to miss the lesson learned with wounds that take time to heal, recovery starts with an understanding that what we have is a gift not a curse, and it deserves our very best energy and time and breath.

It's actually better for you than financial gain. It's more rewarding than mansions and material items. It's better to sit in this than at a wedding or celebration. It's better because we all end up there.

Having said that, I would like to encourage you to do these three things when you're working through your recovery.

Step One: Life is a team sport

You need to invite people into your hurts. Again, when we were created, we were created in community. A triune God created us in his image in a forever relationship with others, this is hardwired into all of us. You are built for relationships. The worst thing you can do in your grief, suffering, and healing is to isolate and try it on your own. That is not to say you don't give yourself time to think and process alone. That is to say you need to invite someone into your hurt, even if they don't understand it.

As I mentioned before, I am a huge fan of counseling. People who are trained and ready to walk through some of the hard stuff alongside you, and push you to a better perspective and outcome. People who give their lives to help people understand their own. These are incredible people who care about their fellow man and woman. You should step into it. It's not taboo, it's not abnormal, and you don't actually have to have a mental ailment to step into it. It's rewarding, revealing, and releasing. Try it. I dare you.

Where you cannot find a counselor, find a trusted friend. Some people cannot find a counselor, but a good friend may be able to step into your hurts with you. It is important though, not to get angry with or place burden upon said friend when they are there to listen and respond. They won't be able to fix it, no one will. But you being alone is not better. Give grace to hear their perspective. Sometimes when you're not feeling the feelings as strongly, you can offer insight that is not seen or known otherwise. They aren't there to hurt you, they are there to help you. Find a friend, dive in.

Hurts and pains are burdens. They can be heavy. It's always better to carry heavy items with others, or you could hurt yourself more. I've thrown out my back before, it's no fun. I encourage you to make sure you don't metaphorically throw yours out by carrying something alone that isn't meant to be carried alone.

Step Two: Find rhythm

I am a big believer in rhythms in life. Disruptions and interruptions to my rhythm are often BIG moments, not little ones, which keep me with some perspective as I live my life. My way of recovery is different from yours, but usually when something hits me big, like this one did, after a season of grief, I get very motivated. And when I am motivated, I create a preferred rhythm to pursue those motivations. When I say that, I mean when I sit in the house of mourning, I actually see my time as more valuable, and particularly how I spend it to be more intentional. It's like it makes me gasp for life all over again. Like that initial rush of air is more present and I'm more aware of it than ever. So I start to prepare a rhythm to intentionally find my way through my days.

I am not a big planner, but I love to work on a plan. I am not a super-organized guy, I'm more creative and free wielding, but a rhythm for me is everything. I am not necessarily at the point that I say I need it, but I can truthfully and honestly say I thrive on it. Get yourself some rhythm, pursue rhythm in your life. How do you do this, you ask? Let me help you.

First, you need to get up at the same time every day. Your sleep patterns are not as necessary as rhythms. Some days you'll sleep in, but if you're sleeping in every day, you're missing out. There's a lot of good stuff out there to go do and see. So, set your alarm, and get up. Oh, yeah, and whatever you set your alarm to in your head just now, set it for thirty minutes earlier, so you can do step two.

Second, begin the day on purpose. I like to move slowly into my days. Before my oldest was born, I would get up around 7 AM every day. My wife would get up much earlier than me. We'd go slow, get a good workout in, and breakfast, and begin the day slowly. I love rolling slow into my days. Having that time of pause. The moment I walk out of my door anything can happen. Literally, anything.

Not sure this works? Remember the last time you missed your alarm and were late to work or school? You threw open your eyes and jumped out of bed. Spent like ten seconds washing your face, brushing your teeth (we hope), and putting on some deodorant in a flash (again, we hope). You rushed over to the last spot you put your keys, and they weren't there of course, they're in your pocket. Then rushing to the car, everyone is driving too slow, and you're looking at the clock while thinking if you could just get some coffee or something things will get better. You race to the parking spot, putting shoes on as you walk into the office, sit at your desk, and realize a sense of relief, because why? Because your day finally will slow down for you to process.

Tell me, is that better? Is that extra thirty minutes of bad sleep better than rolling into your day slower?

My oldest wakes up at 6 AM almost every day. And I have to tell you, some days I wish I could just roll back to sleep. Some days I do. But the majority of the time, he wakes up, and I get up. It takes me about seven minutes to wake up once my feet hit the floor. And in those moments, when he is quietly playing or watching one of his shows, and I'm having a moment of quiet time after a workout, I find myself coming back to life a little bit. Sitting there, staring out the window in a time of quiet allowing my soul to catch up to my body (soul was still in bed apparently). And all at once, I find myself again. Energy coming back. Time is slowing down. More aware of the air in my lungs. Trust me, you want this.

Begin the day on purpose. Don't let it start without you. Get up earlier, get up on time, go slow.

Third, and this one might be most important. The third way to find yourself with some rhythm is to never forget that you have had worse days. You lived through your hardest day, already. Remember that? So, when you do go out the front door and a million things change in a matter of eight or nine hours, never forget that your rhythm cannot be undone by little things, only by big things. If it's a big thing, acknowledge it, and sit in that moment. Allow your rhythm to be thrown off, but only for the right things. But if it's little, don't let it consume your rhythm. Rhythm that is helping you more than hurting you. Rhythm that is keeping you engaged in today, and the time you have left in it. Rhythm that is pushing you to feel the rhythm of the air in your lungs moving up and down. Find your rhythm. Don't let anything throw it off.

Step Three: Trust the pilot

When I was younger I was on a flight. The flight was during the foggiest weather I've ever seen. I'm honestly not sure how we landed. We began our descent and I kept thinking I should see the ground by now. The fog never lifted. I couldn't even tell it apart from the clouds honestly. I began to have a tightness in my chest. Breathing got a little bit heavy and keep in mind, I am not an anxious guy normally. We're coming down, landing gear is opening, and I still can't see the ground. I'm starting to worry a little bit. Then I have this really profound thought that relaxed me as fast as it came into my head.

The thought was simple, "Brent, you're not a pilot."

Are you kidding me? Here I am trying to solve the problems for the pilot that to him or her (cause ladies, I see you) are not problems at all. There was no problem for the pilot. They knew things I didn't. They knew how high we were. They knew the altitude, distance, speed, and location of our final landing space. They knew the direction we were going, and they knew that they were not working with instruments or tools they did not understand. They understood them just fine.

So, here it is. Trust the pilot. Let me explain to you in case you're unsure of Who it is I am talking about. You have to trust God. The Creator of the universe created a universe… he can handle a few details in it. And just in case you're worried that God is not a planner, I'd love to walk you through the scriptures from Genesis to Jesus some time. For now, trust the pilot. Here are two ways you can do that.

The first is to trust the process. Your healing process is a process on purpose. Trust it. Allow yourself to be fully honest during it, and trust the process will see you through. If you're reading this and feel stuck still, it's likely you haven't actually started the process. Start it and trust it. God has got it squared away for your good and the good of those around you.

The second thing you can do, and this is harder for sure, is to trust the plan. I do not know why what happened to you happened. I wish I did. If I did, I'd sleep better at night. But you have to trust the plan. There is a reason this plan is better than your plan. As a matter of fact, a lot of times the plan God has for you is much, much better than the plan you had for yourself.

Do you ever think back to that one time you thought you were going to marry that person? You were young and in love and you did not care who knew it? Then you broke up? And now you are on the other side of things thinking, "Well shucks, I dodged a bullet there." This is why you have to trust the plan. It's better for you. So many people do not trust the plan, and they end up getting themselves into relationships that are not good for them, or will end up putting themselves in situations that are not life giving. This can be avoided. This can be escaped even if you are in one right now. How? By trusting the plan.

Do these two things, and you will be able to see what the pilot has in store for you. Trust that pilot.

To be clear before we move on, as I do not want it to be missed here. The pilot I am referring to is the God of Jesus Christ. The one you read about in the Bible. Not the one you were taught, or the one you heard about from someone else, but rather the one you read about in Scripture. Explore him, get to know him, and trust him. No other pilot is trustworthy. No other pilot is for you as he is.

To learn more, I encourage you to read many of the great works by Lee Stroebel, Francis Chan, John Mark Comer, Andy Stanley, and others. For now, let's work on the next portion of our time and breathing; spending it well.

Chapter 5

DON'T HOLD YOUR BREATH

"The key is in not spending time, but in investing it."
—*Stephen R. Covey*

So, here we are, the actual practical portion of this book. How do we, as a group of people pursue our time and breathing to be utilized to the fullest extent of our intentionality? Another way to say it, how do you fix the problem you have of wasting time?

I believe people when they tell me they are busy. I believe people, even the young people, when they tell me they have a full schedule. You don't have to convince me that people know how to fill their time with all sorts of things that take time.

To be clear, it's incredibly easy to be busy, have a full schedule, and yet get absolutely nothing done for your time. I look at it as a basic return on investment. You put time in, and what you get out of that time is simply the return on the investment for your time. You give an hour, and you will always have something to show for that hour. So my question is why, then, do people constantly look at me and communicate to me that they are out of time? One of the biggest complaints I have from people who are not fulfilled in their lives is the complaint that there just aren't enough hours in the day.

Adding Time

What if it could be done? What if you could add an hour to your day? How much would you pay for it? How much value would that give you? What I get is the complaint that there are just not enough hours in the day, but what if there were enough hours in the day?

Everyone gets twenty-four hours. Nothing changes there. Everyone gets twenty-four hours to make their day complete. There are some pillars in your day that should not be outsourced. You need to shower. Listen to me again, as I say it more clearly, please shower. You need to use the restroom, which ironically, takes time. You need to eat. You need to sleep. You need to talk to people. If you're married, you need to spend time with your spouse, and your kids. You need to make money, you need to spend money.

Contrary to a popular belief that we can isolate and be just fine, you need community. I know what you're thinking, but hear me when I write that I am an introvert. I get it! I get what it's like to need alone time to process, and think, and write, and dream a little bit, and mostly to recover from other people. So, add that time in there too. You need more time, but adding time doesn't actually solve the real problem.

The addition of time only gives an addition of perpetuating a cycle of poor habits of how you spend your time. More accurately, how you spend your breath. I believe that if I gave you an extra hour in your day, you would be prone to waste it on something. Some of you might even waste it by climbing back into the dumb tree.

But let's not leave this thought too quickly, there is a take-away here. You can always add an hour to your day by getting up a half hour earlier and going to bed a half an hour later. But I'm willing to put money on that it is not your addition of your time that needs to be explored.

Allow me to offer you another suggestion as you consider your time. Instead of adding to it, what if you multiplied it?

Paying Attention

I've been pretty adamant through the writing of this book that I am not a fan of the idea of "there aren't enough hours in the day". I said Billion with a B after adding up seconds for thirty-three-year-olds. I get someone to tell me that and I immediately ask them, what are you spending your time on? Remember that question? How are you spending it? Where does your breath get placed?

This is the hardest part of the gig. We need to get really honest about this piece of the puzzle before we can offer any type of possible solutions to your timing woes. How are you spending your time? Not so much asking how are you spending your time in your ideal, but how are you spending your time in your actual? Have you ever asked that question? Have you paid attention to it?

Now, I'm a pastor, no shocker there, as it's been said. And I frequently ask this question to those who tell me they don't have any time, or are stressed out. I work with young people, adults, parents… etc. Unpopular opinion to young people, you're not exhausted. Single moms, or moms of multiple kids are exhausted. Navy Seals are exhausted, but of course they would never admit it. You have more in the tank than you think you do.

People then give me a list out loud. I stop them. I make them take time to write it down. I want to know, and I want them to tell me. Tell me how you're actually spending your time. Tell me where it's going. Give me an idea of how that is actually being spent. Write the hours in the day, tell me when you actually wake up, and when you actually sleep. Tell me your actual schedule. Tell me what you're spending time and energy on. Get granular on this thing. Give me something worth my time to look at and help you through.

And this exercise is one of the best exercises to do. Because it's illuminating. When you find out that you might be wasting time, you worry more about how you spend it.

If you were worried about how you spent your money, and never paid attention to where the money went, you'd overspend on things that are not worth the money all of the time. It's the same concept.

So, do it. Give me an example of how you spend your time. To help, I placed a calendar for one week in this book for you to write in. Or take out a piece of paper, and get writing. There is, however, one rule while writing. Use the last week of your life, and be honest. Do not lie to me and tell me your ideal, tell me your reality. I dare you. Ready? Go.

	Mon.	Tues.	Wed.	Thurs.	Fri.	Sat.	Sun.
12:00 AM							
1:00 AM							
2:00 AM							
3:00 AM							
4:00 AM							
5:00 AM							
6:00 AM							
7:00 AM							
8:00 AM							
9:00 AM							
10:00 AM							
11:00 AM							
12:00 PM							
1:00 PM							
2:00 PM							
3:00 PM							
4:00 PM							
5:00 PM							
6:00 PM							
7:00 PM							
8:00 PM							
9:00 PM							
10:00 PM							
11:00 PM							
12:00 AM							

Don't Hold Your Breath

How was that for you? Was it difficult? Were you honest? What's your schedule look like? Did it work?

Answer me this, are you satisfied? How much television did you watch? How much time did you spend in the shower? How much time did you spend on things that didn't actually afford you more joy and give more life?

For some of you, spending time in front of the TV is a good thing. You need some time to spend sitting, and thinking. But let's not forget that taking care of your body is important as well. I'd wager as well that you need to spend more time with your spouse. I know couples who are married and spend little time together. It's brutal to observe. They have multiple TVs in their home and everyone watches their own thing every night.

What if you substituted that for trying to watch something you both agree on. Or what if you spent time alternating time together watching a show one of you likes, and then the other? Or what if you played a game, poured a glass of wine and engaged in good conversation? Or what if you went on a walk, and tried to engage that pesky one-pound-per-week we talked about in a previous chapter?

Part of not holding your breath with your time is to be honest with how you are actually spending your time. When you write down what gets the majority of your time and what gets the majority of your attention? Are you embarrassed? Are you motivated? Are you bummed? What are you feeling? What if I told you that you don't have to feel poorly about how you spend your time because you are actually able to control that portion of your life?

Part of this chapter is simply pushing into the tension that you're potentially wasting time. You're potentially wasting your breath. The very real and other portion of this section is to give you the opportunity to realize you actually *do* have enough hours in the day, if we spent one less hour watching the show, or one less hour chasing the things that don't give you more life and joy back. This new filter then becomes less about how you're spending your time and more about what does your time bring you? It's less about the hours in the day and more about the air in your lungs. It's less about how you're too busy and more about what you're busy doing.

The truth here is that if you sat down on the couch all of the time, you'd get bored. You'd get bored because you're meant for so much more and created to do so much more than that. You're meant for more than wasting time. You're meant for more than wasting breath. The most efficient people aren't always the smartest people, they are the people who have creatively taken control of the one thing they have control over: how they spend their time. They're the people who have connected something limitless in our minds (like time) to something finite (like the breath in their lungs) and they've managed to not spend it on frivolous living, but rather they've chosen to spend it on something greater and something more intentional.

Multiplying Time

Again, I cannot tell you how many people tell me they have no time, and then I see them spinning their wheels doing things that they don't need to do.

I get most frustrated seeing this in the work environment. Especially when your work matters. Especially when I hear someone who works in the church environment full-time tell *me* that they don't have time. The reason I hate this is because I have the same allotment of time you do, and probably less staff. I seem to get more than my share of things done. So to hear that someone didn't have time to do some of the things they wish they could have, but then you look at their computer and Facebook, instant messenger, email and the like are all pulled up and active. Then you see their phone is on by their computer, and they've been texting the last four hours to their spouse, friends, or kids… etc. I get frustrated because it's just not a true statement that you don't have time. It's that you don't spend your time well. Perhaps you have more time than you realize, and you just don't have the focus of your time you need? Perhaps the perspective of time is that it's endless, and so you waste it on things that don't actually push your main priorities. Then you get into the end of the day and you have nothing to show for your time.

I love to make lists and check them off. I love accomplishing work. I think it was a blessing in the curse of the fall of man, that men (and women) would *have* to work. In this curse of mankind (read Genesis), God didn't have to make work enjoyable. But work can be enjoyable. It can be fun to accomplish the tasks of the day.

So many books have been written about this subject, I dare not presume to go back in and rework great work. I have two favorites you need to read if my last paragraph made you upset with me at all. They'll help you, that is, if you have the time to get help.

The first book is a book called *Indestractable* by Nir Eyal, Julie Li. It's so good! It talks a lot about focus, which this book you are reading spends a little bit of time on. The other book is called *Deep Work* by Cal Newport. Again, another great book that helps you understand how people inadvertently waste time and how you can recapture your time and get more done in less time.

Why does this matter to me and the overall mission of this book? Think about it like this; if this breath that you are breathing right now counts more than anything in the world, if it's the most precious gift you receive today, does that text message you just received really need an immediate response? Does the email really need you to get to it ASAP? Do you need to put this book down and go play with your kid who has been asking for your time?

Maybe we need to take this a bit further. If the air in your lungs might be your last, do you really want to be spending it on *that*? Is that job really the job you were designed for? Is it giving you life? Is it making your heart pound out of your chest? Are you able to connect it to the mission of the Gospel?

It may not be that your work is the wrong environment because after all you need to eat, and so do your kids. Perhaps, you forgot that your work was meant to be on a mission of ushering in the Kingdom of God on earth as it is in heaven. You can do that in the business setting by how you spend your breath and what comes out of your lips when you speak or lead. Perhaps you forgot that your work was meant to be joyful. But when you look at how you spend your time at work, it's easy to see why you have forgotten that. You dread Mondays because you've lost connection to the main reason we show up on Sundays.

We live in a fast-paced, microwave culture where everything needs to be instantaneous. But for years, decades and even a millennia or two, nothing was instantaneous. Such is the other side of the coin of modern technology. What was meant to save us time has created a culture where everything has to be on all of the time and done in an instant, or else we've unleashed a type of fear of missing out we didn't even know existed prior to owning the technology at our literal fingertips.

Now here is the kicker: this fear of missing out is really nothing more than us missing out on things that don't matter in the big scheme of life. They really don't. Do I really need to know what you did last night? Really? How does that affect me, at all? Does it really matter if my favorite sports team won or lost? Really?

If you know me, and read this, you'll know I struggle with waiting. I struggle terribly at times. I love to make a splash, and get immediate results. I'm a millennial and a pastor, so my life is in tension all of the time because of my leadership role within the church. In church organizations, nothing done well is immediate. I often use the phrase "slow is smooth and smooth is fast" to leaders who work with me.

And if we're being really honest, nothing depends on me really. I know that's a big theology conversation about the sovereignty of God and his activity in the world we live in, but I already announced my pastorship many times, so I won't turn back now.

And yet as a millennial, I have a rare tension where I want so badly to make things happen all of a sudden and right now. I want the immediate results so badly. I want them because I love to see things change and maneuver. Some of this because of how I am wired, some of my personality and comfort level with risks.

It is a fun tension I play with in my brain all of the time. Then my pastoral filters start to kick in with simple but hard questions. Why arrive sooner than the journey allows? If you got there faster, would you be more whole or missing something? Great questions to ponder (Side note: I just received a text message while writing this portion of the book, and I had an opportunity to practice what I preached to you in the paragraphs before. I am happy to say I passed the test. Did you?).

Because I am not a guy who likes to wait naturally, and because I love to make a splash (oh, like I'm the *only* one), I have explored for a couple of years what it means to focus my time and energy toward forward momentum. I've done a lot of learning how to focus my time and energy on forward momentum and not sideways energies. I have found that I have a great number of opportunities in this focus which helps me to multiply my time.

So how do we do this well? And what can you do to multiply your time? I'd love to help with that, but let me give you some questions to ponder first.

What are you doing right now in your schedule from a couple of pages ago that you don't really need to be doing? Let me help with that a bit by reminding you: you need to exercise, you need to make money, you need to eat, you need relationships, you need Jesus or at least to take time to explore Him (more on this later). These are non-negotiable. But do you need *that* much exercise? Do you need *that* much money? Do you need *that* many relationships? Is your exploration of Jesus too high or too low?

Did you know that out there, somewhere, right now is a person who would get actual joy from being released to do something that you absolutely hate doing? Did you know that there are people who want to give their first fruits to the Kingdom of God but don't know where to start? Did you know that they are not only easy to find, they're actually remarkably easy to engage as well? It's the beauty of having a multitude of gifts in the world. People are created and wired differently, and that's amazing. I believe that most leaders simply aren't looking for them. I truly believe that. We made a job description and a couple of job requirements our benchmark instead of wiring and gifting. And when they find people who are willing to engage, we assume that those people who are wired specifically for this task know they're invited.

With this in mind, I started doing something years ago as a younger leader that is quite honestly one of the most radical and controversial approaches to ministry I have ever experienced. This is transferable to all of you business leaders as well but I must warn you, it is a little bit out in left field. I have friends who worked at churches who did this so well it changed the footprint and trajectory of the church as a whole and impacted the surrounding communities in mighty ways. I'm going to tell you my secret, but first a warning.

A moment to warn you if you're in the church or business and try this out. My methods are often scrutinized, especially by peers and friends of mine who believe I'm not cut out to lead people the way I do because of how I lead them. They think it's my job to fulfill what only the Holy Spirit can fulfill. But my role as a pastor is to recruit, engage, and release people to do Kingdom work all across our community and within our church. So, before I tell you what I do, ask yourself if you're ready for people to complain about your methods behind your back? Ask yourself if you're really in a position where you believe it is important to multiply your time and focus?

All right, here we go, the practical advice you've been waiting for. In an effort to multiply my time, I asked people to help. That's right, I ask people. Radical! I know it. It's crazy how ridiculous this sounds. I am reading this as I type and I'm thinking to myself, there's no way that could possibly work. I hope you're picking up my sarcasm. Because this paragraph is dripping with it. In the business world this translates as hiring the right positions, or the right people for the positions available without basing it off of qualifications but rather quality of the individual.

Do you remember my conversation in Chapter 3 about being released with my car though? It was exhilarating! I loved it! I felt someone believed in me! When you ask people to join you, you release people to feel that same feeling. I know this feeling, and I will do this, every chance I can.

Let me be clear, I don't randomly ask anyone to serve and I truly wish I could pay everyone with me. I asked people to serve in a specific role to allow myself to accomplish the goals that I felt God had set forward for only me to accomplish by releasing them to tackle things they were uniquely gifted to tackle. And the bummer part, is they do it way better than I do it. It's like a kick in the face with how much better people are at things I'm not good at.

So, when I ask them to help in a specific role, I ask them to commit a certain amount of time for that role. And I encourage them as they learn how to do that role over the timeframe we've agreed upon. It's amazing. (Pro tip: if you find someone absolutely amazing in that role, and you have the budget, hire them. Don't even make them fit a job description. Hire them immediately and help them focus their time by not having to worry about a paycheck from somewhere else.) Why churches feel the need to go into all of the country and find a person for a role that's being filled by someone in their ministry right now is beyond me. But that might be for another book, another time.

In summary, the only way to successfully multiply your time is to get the most out of it. One way to do that is to ask others to join you. Another way to do that is to focus.

Focusing your time should give you a sense of purpose and it should release your time from a constraint to a powerful source of joy in your life. It will give you more peace, and more joy to let down others' expectations of who you're supposed to be and what you're supposed to do and pursue what you're made to do. When you focus on the things that only you can do, it's amazing to see what type of energy you get from them.

I joke with you not, I have to set an alarm to leave work sometimes. I even have to set alarms to stop writing this book. I love it! I have to set alarms to go home from hanging out with the leaders I get to develop. They give me joy. And I *love* being home! I love my wife, my kids, and my old house that always needs something fixed. I love my dogs and my back window that I can look at and enjoy the views from. I love it all. But when I'm in the zone at work, building the Kingdom of Jesus Christ on earth as it is in heaven, man I get jazzed up. I can even wake up early for that job!

They say if you love what you do, you'll never work a day in your life. I say, if you're able to focus on what you do well, you'll never work a day in your life. Loving what you do comes from being able to iron out all of the distractions that pull you away from focussing on what you love to do. I hope and pray you find a way to focus your energy toward that end.

Freedom of honesty

To go forward, we have to chat through a couple of things that give you more freedom than take it away. I can hear it in your thoughts, the argument you're building on why this book is a dud to you. *You don't know my schedule* and *you don't know who I work for* and *if only I had that type of freedom*. I'm going to push back because it's what I do.

You need to have a certain level of honesty with yourself. If you can't do the things you love because you *have* to do all of the things you don't love, then I would argue you're in the wrong position or wrong environment. Or perhaps you have the wrong understanding of your role in that environment or what accomplishes a win for you and your organization. For me, the win is very simple: help people take one step closer to God. Which means I win every time I make you think about God just a little bit. Hopefully with this book, I've won multiple times. And if you finish the book, I know I'll win at least once in Chapter 7. The freedom of honesty is profound. Because I can honestly spin my wheels and on my best day, not accomplish my win.

It gives you freedom to choose your requirements by knowing how you're winning is impacted by the day. I could create the most amazing spiritual moment of your life, and do the work on a lot of things and have no one show up. I could create the perfect set up for you to encounter Jesus and create moments that bring tears to your eyes. I could send letters, emails, information, social media posts, text messages, but at the end of the day it could go completely wrong. Especially if you look at my life and think my life isn't lining up with my words or actions. The honesty about my role in the church is that I have no control over what happens. So why waste time doing anything that doesn't help usher people toward the Gospel?

This is my point. You're not being honest. You're spending time and energy on things that don't matter. And you're blaming others for it. I've said no to meetings that won't get me closer to the mission I'm trying to accomplish. And it has frustrated people, and coworkers. But I don't need to be in those meetings, they do.

For some of you, you're spending time and energy chasing a position or a spot in a hierarchy that you believe will make you a better, more prominent leader and believing a lie that someone told you somewhere along the way that if you arrive there, you'll have made it to your potential. But I would argue that if you focus your time and energy on the things that really matter, you'll have more joy, peace, patience, kindness, goodness, gentleness, and self control. More on this later. If you cannot be honest with yourself, you'll never experience these freedoms.

Freedom Schedule

When I was in college, I had a system to accomplish all of my schooling. To put my time in perspective for you so that you know my schedule. I took fifteen to eighteen credit hours a semester, worked about twenty-five to thirty hours a week at a local restaurant (four days a week x five to nine hours a shift), and had enough time to volunteer for a couple of things my first two years of college, and then entered into an internship program at a church fifty minutes from the campus to work as a student ministry intern for about twenty hours a week. Throw in the physical activities I was doing, playing soccer with friends three or four nights a week, many lunches with friends, and all of the Call of Duty I could play; I was a busy guy. Did I forget to mention that I was having amazing quiet times, running almost six miles a day a couple of times a week and still enjoying a lot of time for social engagements? Thriving!

To say I had a full schedule was and is an understatement. Here is the craziest thing; I loved it. Put a lot of emphasis on the word *loved*. Because I *loved* it, so much. I was thriving! I had no one to worry about but myself, and I managed to do a lot of things in my hours. I studied hard, worked hard, played hard, laughed hard, "Call of Dutied" hard, and all in the in-between. I slept hard, too. All of this made possible because somewhere in my late freshman year or early sophomore year I realized a couple of secrets to my ability to do all of these things. I'll give them to you here.

First, I had to get organized. Now I am not a traditionally organized person. Hear me the right way, I love organization and organized people. People who naturally and efficiently organize are my heroes in a lot of ways. My wife is one of these people. She organizes my life. She puts things in places she knows I'll find them when I need them. At the time, though, I didn't have a wife. I had me. And I had a me who is Type B and not crazy organized. This is a bad combo for people who have a lot going on. So, the main purchase I would make every semester would be a couple of different notebooks for school, and a calendar. I needed a calendar. I bought one notebook per semester and it would help me organize my life. I would get the college ruled five subject notebooks. And each subject was in order to the time of the day it came in my schedule. I would use this until it went empty, and then reload.

Then I had my calendar. And I had to write things down. Google calendar eventually came into my life, and boom, an organized schedule is something I've lived on for years. I did this by creating healthy habits to help me organize my schedule.

So, I got organized and here is how. I block scheduled. There are some things I couldn't miss. I could miss the occasional soccer night with my friends, but I had to go to class. Say it with me, students, *I have to go to class.* Going to class made it easier for me to learn. I learn by doing but I retain information by hearing and writing. It comes natural to me, so I don't try to fight the wave, I just ride it. I went to class. I didn't distract myself in class, I paid attention. Now my block schedule looks different, but there are still the same principles in my life.

I have to go to work, there is no denying that. I have to study scripture and theology. I have to study culture, and make sense of a world that doesn't make sense. Here's a recently added block for the last couple of years in my schedule; I have to think. I need time to process.

Add these requirements to the reality that I have to also write sermons, perform weddings, have strategic and vision meetings, develop leaders, pastor people, as well as work within the programmatic elements of my role and there are some things I cannot skip. Now, keep in mind, I'm a pastor, so I also *have* to spend some time with just God, in the quiet. I could make a very compelling case that everyone has to spend some time coming to grips with God in the quiet, but maybe that is another different book. How many other books are we at now? I have to spend that time. These blocks go in first.

Another block that is becoming more and more important to me the older I get and higher I go in the influence I have with people around me is that I have to take a sabbath. I have to slow down, once a week, for a whole twenty-four-hour period and spend time enjoying the presence of God. I have to not work for a whole day. There are a couple of authors who write on this, but John Mark Comer's *Ruthless Elimination of Hurry* and *Garden City* are easily two of the most influential writings I've come across on this subject, at least for me.

The last block of my day is the block of time between when I get home and my kids go to bed. I have to block this time off. Nothing is more important to me than this family time that lasts only a precious few hours. I can check my emails again when everyone is sleeping, for this moment, I need to wrestle my boys and kiss my wife. I need to be present and not somewhere else mentally. I need to block it off.

Why do I tell you all of this? Because you need to get organized. If you presently struggle to keep everything in line with your day, or find yourself forgetting things, or even feel overwhelmed, you need to get organized. So get organized, and block off the most important things you do first.

Second, I found that I needed to get a head start. Once or twice a semester I would spend a large chunk of time in a day at the library. I found out that if I started working ahead, I could actually get a lot of my course work done before it was actually due. Usually it meant being in the library for a full Saturday from sun up to dinner time. I would get there and crank work out. This was a game changer! I would be about midway through the semester and have all of my coursework done minus one or two items. Those were usually bigger items that I didn't know how to do yet. By doing this, I freed up a lot of my time during the week.

It blew my mind to watch people struggling with having three exams and five papers due all in the same week. Here I am studying for the exams and tweaking papers instead of starting from scratch. It was amazing to experience how little stress I incurred during this time. I saved myself from a lot of future gray hairs, I hope. It was so worth one Saturday a semester. It worked for me.

The last thing I had to do was get really disciplined. To help me get there, I made some rules for myself. I remember learning about the importance of rhythm and routine, so I woke up every day at the same time, no matter how much or how little sleep I had gotten. I found rhythm in my daily schedule, my class schedule and my night schedule. I found that I thrive on freedom of a full schedule and time well spent, so I would load classes on Tuesdays and Thursdays. To put it into context in my current role, I try to get all of my meetings to land on one day a week. It doesn't always play out, so there are two days a week that my meetings land. I try to get them out of the way so my brain and schedule aren't bogged down.

I set my schedule and will keep it minus the one-off moments that come up randomly. I don't work on Saturdays. Occasionally, there will be a big thing at our church that I will need to be a part of, but I don't work on Saturdays.

People don't even text me anymore on Saturdays about work stuff, and I have to tell you, that is amazing to have.

Discipline is the more important practice of this chapter. You have to have discipline. When you have these three things happening all at once, you experience freedom. Freedom of an honest look at your time and how you spend it, freedom of a full schedule and the freedom of time well spent. Because, after all, this whole book is about you spending your time better. This book is about you harnessing the breath in your lungs for your better. Maybe you're wasting too much time because you're not disciplined with it?

Dig in, and get it done

It's time for you to dig into your calendar, schedule, and priorities and get some things done. Some of you have put it off for too long. You would rather binge watch a show, or spend time doing absolutely nothing and wasting time and breath on things that get you nowhere. And I have to tell you, it's mind-numbing. You know this to be true. It's certainly not everything you wanted life to be. But perhaps the circumstances are not against you, you're just not working the circumstances to your favor?

This is a paradigm shift. If you're a Christian, by that I mean, if you have a dependent relationship on the death and resurrection of Jesus as it comes into the context of your sin (more on this in Chapter 7), then you have an obligation to spend your time better. I might even argue it is your first calling. Go into the world and preach the Gospel, baptizing them in the name of the Father, Son, and Holy

Spirit. These are two action statements. Hopefully, you can spend your time doing, instead of doing nothing.

So this is your charge. This is your battle cry. This is the push. This is the sign you've been waiting for. Get up, dig in, and get it done. Get moving. Get out there and start breathing. You never know, if you do this the right way, you might find yourself out there, somewhere, actually living.

Chapter 6

TRULY FREE

"For to be free is not merely to cast off one's chains,
but to live in a way that respects and enhances
the freedom of others."
—Nelson Mandela

Think of a time you were the most free you've ever been. Think of a time when you experienced the most freedom-like feelings in your world. What were those times? I remember certain moments of freedom in my life that I have enjoyed, but one of the times I have felt and feel the most free in my life are the times I get a chance to go rock climbing.

If you've never been rock climbing, it's a thrilling and challenging experience. You and the rock are at odds with each other and yet work in tandem to face off against gravity. You must work with and against the rock to stay engaged in a battle of strategy and strength and dexterity. Rock is a sturdy medium in which to face off against gravity. It's a constant. But isn't it interesting that the times I feel the most free are the times that I have the most constraints on me? In this particular case, I mean that literally.

There is this cultural phenomenon I'm observing in the world, that freedom is this constraint-free environment in which your bliss and happiness are combined in an amazing utopia of being free from constraints, pressures, and any outside forces. But isn't it true that to enjoy freedom, you have to submit to some constraints? Without those constraints your freedom can spiral into chaos, and that never ends well for anyone. Let's take rock climbing as an example.

I enjoy rock climbing so much but there are certain factors at play. The first is gravity. How great is gravity? Isn't it true you don't even notice gravity until you and gravity are working against each other? Or for some of you, you noticed gravity in sports. Why can't I dunk that basketball? Why can't I block the net? Why can't I jump higher, run faster? Maybe you need some P.F. Flyers that Benny "the jet" Rodrigues had in the movie, *The Sandlot*? Dating myself? Maybe.

Yet, gravity is a constraint. It pushes against you and holds you down, literally and thankfully. The interesting thing is that without it, we'd be floating in the air never to return to the ground again. And don't even get me started on center of gravity without gravity. So I would argue gravity is a good thing as it keeps you grounded. That's a double meaning of the word there and I like it.

Gravity acts against you. Yet you don't ever complain about it, minus the skinned knee here and there. Even then, you probably didn't blame gravity. It was probably your two left feet. Which is something you should get in a record book for or get it checked out.

Then there is the harness. Yes, I said harness. I'm not one of those dudes who goes out there without it. The harness is a constraint designed to hold you in and up. The design of the harness is to keep your body from plummeting to the ground to certain injury or death when you lose your hold or gravity takes over. It's a constraint that is there for your safety. It's actually good for you. No one would sit back and think negatively about that harness when it's saving your life. You may not like how it feels when you fall, but you're glad you were caught.

For the purest climbers in the world, who would prefer to climb without one, they would communicate differently with a vision that is great for them, but for the vast majority of us, wearing that harness allows us to even begin the climb. At the same time, they would argue with clarity that they accept the consequences of the first constraint, gravity. Remember that one?

Add in the rope, carabiners, and even the belay systems. All working as constraints that can seem limiting, but all working together to fight against gravity's pull on you.

So, why the lesson in constraints? Isn't it true that all freedom comes with some constraints? Perhaps, maybe even the best freedoms come with some constraints. The ones that actually make you believe you're free, come with some sort of acting force that puts in boundaries for you. Yet, we get frustrated when our lives have them. We get frustrated because we look at those constraints as a negative thing. May I encourage you to change your perspective and help you to see them as a positive influence in your life?

The truth is, you'll never truly experience freedom in some of the things in this world without submission to some constraints. So, freedom needs a different filter as we process it.

Intolerance

Intolerance is one of the ways we have the opportunity to engage in freedom. Sometimes engaging in freedom is eliminating the unnecessary boundaries in your life. To become intolerant of something is to be unwilling to accept the views, behavior, or belief surrounding that something. Intolerance in culture today has become this big buzz word that often pushes you into the camp of bigotry or closed-mindedness, but let's look at the facts of what is and isn't intolerant and why it matters.

I'm a musician in some respects. I can strum an acoustic guitar pretty well, and I enjoy it. In the world of music, intolerance is actually a main feature, though artists may never say this out loud. It is intolerant to play a G note as a C note. In this regard, by the law of non-contradiction, a G note is a G note and nothing else. There is no other way around that. It is an intolerant world in the music world. One we don't settle for anything less than perfection in.

Yet when we hear the voices, listen to the songs, engage with the beauty of such an intolerant world, it actually gives us enjoyment. Music perfectly intertwined together to produce something new, beautiful, and albeit enjoyable is a true testament to the intolerance of the craft. Have you ever gone to a bad concert and wondered why it sounded so muddy? Would you really be cool with spending the big money on something we expect to be perfect? You find yourself at a garage band concert, your expectation is low. But if you showed up to see, say, Harry Styles, Ed Sheeran, Justin Bieber, or other professional singers, songwriters, or performers, they better be throwing down some intolerance on their music.

Play with good-enough musicians, and they'll actually let you know if one of your strings is out of tune or if you hit a wrong note. Because there is a way that the note of *G* sounds and anything else is not right. It doesn't hit the mark. It falls short. And what do we do with that intolerance? We love it! We thrive on it. We buy it! Musicians strive for it. They reach for the stars with it.

It's illogical and frankly uninformed to think intolerance is a bad thing in this respect. Intolerance is actually a good thing. And ultimately that intolerance leads to music. Music we would not accept as anything other than in its perfect form. I'll take this a bit further. We don't love bad musicians. Unless they are your kid, of course. And while we're on the subject, you're right, I'm sure they're really good. But the rest of us won't put them on a pedestal and praise their abilities if they aren't any good. We say, "not good enough" and move on.

How rude! What bigoted closed-minded thinking, us wanting musicians to be great at what they do.

So, intolerance can be a very good thing when we frame it in the right way. Taking it a step further, we should be intolerant of injustices in the world. We should not tolerate the human injustices of racism, or sexism. No one should be looked down upon because of the color of their skin, where they are from, or what they were born into with regards to their gender. They don't get to choose those things (I stand by this statement across the board). Somehow, though, we have shifted the intolerance debate to that of social preferences, instead of human justices, which is how I think the whole thing got muddied up in the first place.

The most common blame goes to people who follow Jesus. However, from what I read of the historical context of scripture is that it was indeed Jesus who elevated the minorities and the least-seen people in culture. As a matter of fact, it would be difficult not to follow any human justice movement to anything but a value upheld by the teachings of Jesus. Honestly, try it. I'd love to see it happen. But as we continue this book, let's not get lost in my poor ability to be politically correct or unbiased. Let's instead continue down the row of pursuing how we spend our breath and how that intertwines with our freedom.

The Samurai Effect

Intolerance is an important piece of the puzzle as we talk about this next part, which I would call the Samurai Effect portion. I was first introduced to this ideology through the movie with Tom Cruise called *The Last Samurai*. Have you seen it? Here's a synopsis.

Tom Cruise plays a character who is a drunkard and engaged in war with the Samurai nation. He eventually finds himself their captive after an engagement. Throughout that captivity, while the Samurai learn about their enemy, Tom Cruise's character is learning about them. He then realizes the slower, intentional, dedicated lifestyle is worthy of emulating, and begins to try to train with them.

He begins to question: "What does it mean to be Samurai? To devote yourself utterly to a set of moral principles, to seek the stillness of your mind, and to master the way of the sword?" He goes on earlier in the film, "From the moment they wake, they devote themselves to the perfection of whatever they do." When I hear statements like this, something in me aches and groans for that type of honor and devotion. Do you feel the same? It's beautiful in every respect. The discipline to have honor and devotion intertwined.

Taken further, the word Samurai means to serve. In practice they would serve a higher calling, or a higher purpose. It means to take on your master's vision and bleed for it. You may even die for it. And to do that, would be honorable and great. To truly engage with it. And wouldn't you know that gave more purpose and life to the Samurai than fighting over competing visions or trying to live their lives in a certain way?

What is your vision?

So let me ask you the question: what is your vision you're chasing? What are the competing visions to that vision? What if you could capture the opportunity to be truly free and breathe deep breaths? To take your days and devote yourself to a set of moral principles? What would it look like for you to be unwavering in the way you treated people? To be unmoved by any circumstances in your character? To be able to stand for only our own moral code and not be tossed around by the wind and the waves?

What would it look like to seek the stillness of your mind? To process what is best for you, and those you love most, by making decisions from a quiet mind, as opposed to the loud chaotic one? What would it look like for you to step into that stillness and drink deep from the well of it? Could you spend time in a relaxed state and make moves and decisions from that mindset toward something existential instead of something trivial? I believe you can do this.

What if you could master the way of the sword? Did you know that Paul, the writer of Ephesians, wrote about the Word of God (aka the Bible) as the sword of the Spirit? It's actually something you can master. And you aren't even required to believe in it to master it! Though I admit, it would be difficult to not do both of those things combined.

Here is the kicker, and where the tension lies really, you cannot do any of these things with a jam-packed schedule filled with nonsense getting you nowhere. You also cannot do any of these things without intentionality. After all, to master something requires a lot of what? You guessed it correctly! It requires a lot of your time. It requires a lot of your breath. It costs you something to do this well, but it will cost you way less in the long run, I promise you that.

So, if you would allow me to, I would like to take one more shot at helping you be able to do these things. I would love one more chance to invite you to explore the one area of your life that really is worth your time exploring. It may be the only thing worth your time. I'd like you to explore Jesus.

Your Next Step

It may be difficult to move on from here because you decided a long time ago to not explore Jesus. Maybe you've written him off in your life. You made a decision at thirteen years old, or twenty-three, or twenty-four, or forty, or even sixty, to write off the Jesus thing. But let me ask you this, now that you're older, what else are you still doing that you were doing at those ages?

You probably look back at those ages, and because of the experiences you have had, you could look back and give some pretty solid advice in hindsight about how to utilize time, certain opportunities, and even possibilities. So why do you still take advice from the twelve-year-old version of yourself on this matter? If Jesus is who he said he is, it matters more than anything else in the world. Everything else in your life has grown up over time, maybe your understanding and exploration of who Jesus is needs to as well.

Chapter 7

ENJOY THE LIFE

"We must be free not because we claim freedom,
but because we practice it."
—*William Faulkner*

"I am the way, the truth and the life."
—*Jesus Christ*

I had a friend who told me he only reads the first and last chapter of each book. So if that is true, and he actually reads this book, Matt, this chapter is for you. (No, I didn't use his real name... or did I? *We* may never know, but *he* will know.)

If this book were a song, this is the crescendo. This is what this book is all about. I don't think there is any secret by now if you've made it this far in the book that I am pointing you toward something really important. Something that is worth your time. Something that is worth your breath. I put it at the end, because it is a great way to measure your commitment to exploring the long-game goals we talked about in Chapter 1 and the prologue. I truly hope you made it. And if you're reading this, then you know you're committed to finishing and finishing strong. Don't be afraid. You're almost there!

Marathons

In my experience, the most valuable trait of any marathon finisher is that they began with the goal to finish. Many marathoners have a time slot in their minds, but when the gun goes off, and you're running your first marathon, every good coach calls you to focus on finishing, over your time. Why do they do it? Because running a marathon is hard! It's really hard. It is mental as much as it is physical. But if you don't set your goals, your mind will tell you, before your body does, that the goals you set aren't reachable. And if your mind tells you that enough, and you believe it, you may not finish.

I can't think of anything more worth your time than to explore the person and story of Jesus Christ. Why is this chapter in this book? I'm unapologetically a pastor, remember? I admitted that at the very beginning and throughout. But hopefully, if I have kept you this long, you're invested enough to at least finish the book. I also hope you know that with all of the things I've tried to teach in this book, there is one core foundation to all of the "why" questions. And here it is: if Jesus is who he says he is, it is worth your time to explore what that means. In this chapter I'll give you a brief overview of who Jesus is, and why I believe that he's worth exploring. Then I'll give you my reasoning for connecting the dots and trying to maximize my time.

This next smaller section won't read like me, but it's the quickest way I could get you all of the content you needed to know without putting too much flowery speech into the conversations. It's worth your time to explore each of these individual situations at a much more invasive scale, but if you don't believe in Jesus, frankly, it won't matter. It's not that they aren't important, but they all point to, and revolve around, one person in particular. His name was Jesus. So here we go.

Back to the Beginning

Do you remember in Chapter 2 when I introduced you to how God created man? Well, when he created men and women in His own image, God gave them a mandate of sort, or a mission: work the land and have dominion over it and enjoy this life. I guess that's kind of two or three mandates. God placed the two in a garden where he would walk with them. Read it has history, poetry or folklore, keep the main point in front, God's original design for man was for us to be created in his image and to live in his presence. It was better than the most amazing thing you've ever seen. More peaceful than we'll ever know this side of heaven. It may not have been the view that created tranquility, but rather the presence of God that dwelt among the view that really pushed it into astronomical beauty.

God gave them one rule, don't eat of one particular tree. I encourage you to read the story in Genesis 3 as we follow the account of the serpent who lured them into eating of the tree. Here is the problem we face when we discuss this moment in humanity. We think to ourselves, how could they have been so stupid? And yet, we all have been there (remember the dumb tree?).

I think more obvious than the giving into temptation is a question that haunts me: why were they even close to it?

In Genesis 3, God gives them dominion over an entire garden. Don't think it was like your backyard, think like a rain forest.

Yet they were around the tree. They had already taken a step toward the danger zone before tempted in the danger zone. Insert sermon about why good guardrails on your life matter more than you know.

Here is the truth: in perfect conditions, we're prone to choose ourselves, our wants, our desires, our temptations, over something that is ultimately better for us. If that sounds like a leading statement, it is. In perfect conditions, we're prone to waste our breath on things that aren't better for us even though they may seem to be. Keep reading.

So, they eat from the tree, and in that moment, there is a shift in every relationship we hold. There was a debt created in every relationship. This debt couldn't be repaid by us. There had to be something or someone to repay it. And to repay it, the conditions had to be perfect. With that in mind, I'll take you through each debt very briefly.

Relationship with God

Scripture describes a relationship with God with the Hebrew word *shalom*. Shalom is defined as peace, tranquility, or harmony. In our relationship with God as human beings, God and man were in perfect shalom. Imagine the way your hands fit each other. Fingers perfectly intertwined to fit your hands. Or imagine something that fits perfectly, like a Lego piece microscopically designed to connect (This sentence was for you, Jake.) Shalom was available and we lived in perfect shalom with God.

When the fall of man happened (i.e., Adam and Eve breaking the one rule), shalom was broken. Sin entered the world, and with it death. This is a very important piece of the puzzle for when we talk about why Jesus needed to come. More on that later in this chapter. Your debt was created by your sin. This debt was inherited with the realities of your humanity.

With shalom broken, soon to follow was a chosen people, a law and a covenant with Abraham (see the old testament for details). So shalom was broken, and in its place came tension or a gap in shalom. We no longer had access to God's presence because of our sin and disobedience. God's holiness couldn't be in shalom with such unholiness. Thus the debt was created and persists to this day between man and God. But that's not the only debt we feel, in real time, in our culture today.

Relationship with Men and Women

Shalom was also broken between men and women. This makes so much sense to you if you think logically. Name one person you always get along with without any type of tension. Name one. Shalom broken between men and women meant tension would come and go in those relationships. Though it's a beautiful thing that tensions can be resolved, it still permeates relationships.

Even the best marriages you know have tensions. In our default setting we're prone to think of ourselves first, remember? Great marriages and relationships you know work very hard to put themselves second, therefore doing the best they can to recapture an imperfect amount of shalom on this side of heaven. This is unable to be completely done without the help of Jesus who teaches the idea that you are not here on this earth for just you, but that's still coming.

Relationship with Life and the Earth

When shalom was broken at the fall, we also had a break in shalom with our relationship with life and the Earth. With life, it's simple to explain; we all die. That's a definite break in our relationship with life that was originally designed for eternal shalom with God.

Once more, the earth would have to be toiled. Something that was once a joyful and effortless undertaking given to us by God's provision without too much toilsome work, would need to be cultivated and toiled over to produce minimum fruit. I'm at the point in my theology to believe that not even weeds existed in the garden with Adam and Eve until the fall of man, because who can possibly take joy from pulling weeds? Seriously, Grandma, tell me who?

Relationship with Community

Shalom was broken among the community. People see things their own way, again in selfishness. The harmony of a community was broken. I don't believe I have to wrestle this one to the ground. Look around at culture today and tell me we're living harmoniously in our communities. It's not possible. The racial tensions, the demographic tension, the tensions and disparities in education, quality of life, and so on. Our communities are wrecked.

And yet, there are some communities that seem to thrive in their unbelievable amount of diversity. Who is at the center of those? Yes. The perfect Sunday school answer goes here: Jesus.

The Need for a Savior

So this break of shalom created a need. A need for a Savior. If you follow through the Old Testament, you'll see a unique journey to get to Jesus. The first situation we see is the law being created. God chooses a people (Israel) through whom he would rescue out of slavery and take them on a journey toward Him. These people would receive the law, ten commandments, anyone? They would receive the laws as a confirmation of being God's chosen people, not a condition of it.

They would be judged, receive prophets, get kings, lose kings, get more prophets, get more information, and they would live their lives in a bilateral covenant which basically says, you do this, and God will do that.

Part of the bilateral covenant required a blood sacrifice designed to repent. Since the fall of man, death entered the world; only through death could a sin be redeemed. So, there was an actual system in the law to explain which payment went with which sin. Typically a goat, pigeon, ox, or a lamb. These sacrifices needed to be the best of the best, flawless, and unblemished.

This all leads to a moment in history when God had sent a ton of information to a people and set the table for something more that He was doing. All of this prepared the way for the Savior of the Earth to come forth.

Important note for quality control: thinking logically, in order to receive a Savior, you need something to be saved from. Since the definition of the word sin means to fall short, it provides us a better understanding of what we are falling short from. We fall short from a standard of good required to pay the debt we are in. But I have good news, there was someone who fit the requirements.

Good God

You hear it said a lot probably, that God is good. CS Lewis wrote about this in his writings often. The reality of that statement is this: if God is good, then nothing else can be. Because if God is the definition of good, God defines goodness, and if the measurement of what is good is God, then anything that falls short of God falls short of good. Which means, if God is good, no one else is. Since we all fall short and we all sin, then we cannot be good. We need a good God to meet us where we're at, because we cannot measure up.

And this is how good our God is. When shalom was broken and the debt was created, it could only be paid back by a spotless lamb. What do I mean by that? The sacrifice of payment had to be as good as God. The righteousness of God had to be without blemish. Since God is the only one who fits the requirements needed to pay the debt, God created a way for us to get it back with him. Insert the story of Jesus.

Jesus is a Real Person

Here we are! You made it! Insert Jesus story here. With shalom broken between God and man, a law that was impossible to follow indicating a need for a Savior, and a debt that was impossible for us to pay on our own, God stepped in and made our salvation personal. He sent his Son, Jesus.

God sent Jesus (fully God and fully man) to Earth to be what we could never be: righteous. Jesus came not to add to the law, but to fulfill the law (Matthew 5:17-20). Now this is a huge statement. One that Jesus himself made. You know this now after the last couple of pages. In order to fulfill the law, one would have to never break the law. And the only way to fulfill a law you never broke was to be the payment for the debt of that broken law. So, Jesus lived his life in fulfillment of the law and He would come to be the ultimate sacrifice. The debt of our breaking of the law could be taken off of our shoulders as a burden to us and paid for by Jesus in full. After all, Jesus is often referred to as the Lamb of God throughout Scripture.

So, Jesus comes and lives his life in holiness, righteousness, and shalom with God. He then gets into his ministry in his thirties and starts to stir a ruckus amongst the people by claiming to be like God and to be God. John, the best friend of Jesus, connected this statement in his letter to the Gentiles: "In the beginning was the Word [Jesus], and the Word [Jesus] was with God, and the Word [Jesus] was God. He [Jesus] was with God in the beginning" (John 1:1-2).

This is why it is so important to explore Jesus. This is why it matters. There is no one in the history of the world effectively arguing against the reality that Jesus lived on this Earth. The reason for this is because it's not just the written documents compiled as the Bible that they have to contend with. There are historical figures, including a very prominent Jewish historian named Josephus, who write about Jesus. He's a real person.

Once more, recall the authors who wrote what is now known as the Bible did not know they were writing a Bible. The Bible was written by witnesses who took an account of what they saw. At first, it was a collection of historical writings and highly valued accounts. As a matter of fact, Luke wrote in his Gospel that many had written down an account of this guy from Nazareth we know as Jesus. Many took Jesus' life down and wrote about it because of what happened. So the question of whether Jesus lived is not a measure of if you believe the Bible or not, it's actually an account of if you believe the writers who were there or not.

When you spend time exploring the history behind the person of Jesus there is only one conclusion to whether or not he lived on this Earth, and was crucified. It's undeniable.

Now if Matthew, Mark, Luke, or John are reliable sources for the story of what happened, all of whom were written about by other historians as well, then there might be something to the story of Jesus that is worth looking into. You see, if Jesus is who Jesus said he was, then that is worthy of a look.

It is worth your time, and your breath, to explore this Jesus who has more evidence to support his reality than there is opinion to try to dispute it.

Jesus, a true story

We're here! Hurray! We're at the best part of the story. Jesus spends three years in his thirties proclaiming really crazy things like love God and love your neighbor. He switches the mentality of the time to produce a different paradigm by how people think about who God is, and what the purpose of His Kingdom brought to the Earth is.

He started being so countercultural that people started to actually believe in the message he was preaching. Repent from your sins, and trust in Jesus. He did this so effectively by performing miracles, fulfilling prophecies given hundreds of years before he entered the scene, and helping people along the way by performing signs and wonders like healing the sick, helping the blind see, and forgiving people of their sins. The problem was he was doing all of this on the sabbath and drawing attention from people who didn't like that he was becoming famous in the land.

They loved him so much, they murdered him. Yes that is to be read dripping with sarcasm. They killed him. They nailed him to the cross. Awesome way to go, huh? He was crucified.

This is the scary part. Jesus called this. This is where the true story comes in. Jesus called it. He knew this was going to take place, explained it was going to take place, and then when it took place, people didn't believe it was actually taking place. Jesus knew that there was one way to pay the debt for us created by us at the fall of man. The only way to pay the debt was for him to pay it. He willingly paid for it. He was crucified for your sin, for your falling short. He died to pay your debt. And the kicker is, the story doesn't end there.

Jesus, a faith story

This is my hands-down favorite part of the story of Jesus. Jesus was crucified. You can be sure of that because it was the Roman Empire that crucified him, and in this time, the Romans were good at a lot of things, and killing people is one of them. Also, if you like connecting dots, check out some of the prophecies about Jesus being pierced for our transgressions but remaining unbroken then peek at his death on the cross and what happened when they went to take him down. It's pretty gnarly.

So, Jesus was taken down from the cross and put into a tomb. In front of that tomb a very heavy stone was rolled in the doorway. This was probably two-fold, to keep others out, and to keep the smell in. There's nothing fun about a body rotting.

My favorite part of the story is here. At that moment, the same disciples who had followed Jesus for a long time, went into hiding because they thought the story was over. Jesus was dead, and they went home. Weird, right? Especially when we read in John, Luke, Mark, and Matthew about what happened. Why would guys, who were told the game plan and wrote a lot of the accounts we read in the New Testament, actually not believe in the story they were told was going to happen? It's because it hadn't happened yet. And sometimes, seeing is believing. This is why I love this part.

So, Jesus is in the tomb, and some of the ladies who loved him (think friends and family, not girlfriend or wife) and knew him, who are in mourning by the way, decide to head toward the tomb to care for the body. This is the modern day comparative to visiting a grave to put flowers on the tombstone. They were going to go and do their best to try to preserve the body of Jesus as long as possible with oils, spices, and fragrances. You read that correctly, the dead body of Jesus. But when they arrived, the stone was rolled away and the grave was empty! Insert the intense orchestra swelling of a tense and suspenseful tone in the movie.

The grave was empty, and they did what anyone would do in that situation, they immediately started preaching the Gospel. Actually this is kind of true and false.
They ran back to their friends, including the guys, because you would too! And they shared, for the first time ever, without even knowing it or piecing it all together, the story of an empty grave where Jesus was supposed to be lying dead. They shared the good news, and they didn't even know it was good news! Jesus' body was reduced to flesh and bone (that is, lacking breath) and was now nowhere to be found. Nobody was expecting no body!

Why I believe it

This is why I believe in this story. It is so far out there that there is no way to believe in this story outside of taking into account the testimony of the people who were there. Now, if it were just one or two people, there is not much validity, as people can tell a good story. In contrast, any religious organization that centers around the words of one person, is not a religion worth following in my educated experience. That is what makes this particular story so great.

The simple fact, this story is not a story that would have made it past the first century if it didn't happen. Here is a glimpse of the evidence I have observed and studied over the years.

We don't have one eye witness telling this story, we have many eye witnesses. It goes beyond the four books of the Gospel as well. Luke records in Luke 1:1-2 that "*Many* have undertaken to draw up an account of the things that have been fulfilled among us, just as they were handed down to us by those who from the first were eyewitnesses and servants of the word." Did you catch that? Many people. Not a couple, not even some, but many!

Not only that, but Jesus wasn't famous at all. So, why would many people write an account of his actions in his thirties? Why have you heard about him 2000 years later? How many people have taken into account your life story? Let's take that question more intentionally. How many people have taken into account your birthday, and just over roughly three years of your life, written multiple copies of your life story? How many? Probably not many.

Why does this matter? If that many people were taking down the events that happened in the day, then it's fair to postulate that many other people were carefully considering any accounts of what happened and would quickly dispute them if they were not true or squash them. They wouldn't just dispute them, they would squash it fast! It would not even have made it past the first century.

Then think about how many people on opposite sides of the belief system would have to corroborate a story for it to hold true for so long. Then think about people. We cannot even get our States in the US to agree on things, or any group really to that point. I mean, have you been to a board meeting of any kind lately? It can be taxing to find unity.

It's like this. What if I told you I could fly, but really couldn't fly? I know, you're bummed! But if I told you I could fly, and wrote my own book about me flying, you likely wouldn't believe it without witnesses. So then let's say I got a bunch of people to lie for me. I paid them, or coerced them with my niceness or charm and they all agreed. If all I had was one witness, I wouldn't be too trustworthy. If I had a million witnesses, who have never seen me fly, it wouldn't be trustworthy.

However, if I actually could fly (I can't, but stick with me here) and people saw me do it and wrote down what they saw without coercion or any type of manipulation from me. All they did was write down what they saw and made sure to record it. Then, if people didn't just write down what they saw, but made detailed accounts of where I did it, when I did it, and how I did it, then there would be some legs to the witness accounts.

Take it further. If those same people who saw me fly, started telling others about me flying, and they were all saying the same thing, and someone overheard them telling the story and said "I saw that too" and so on and so forth, we would still be gaining ground to the case that it actually happened.

The difference between my analogy and Jesus is simple, Jesus' body still hasn't been recovered to this day. Like, no one knows where it is, all that we know is that just like my wallet, it isn't where we left it.

This is the most ironclad evidence to me. Jesus walked the earth, fact! No one is arguing this. Jesus performed miracles, fact! No one who was there is arguing about this. Jesus had many eye witnesses who were there at said miracles performed and said walking the earth, fact! If Jesus didn't do these things, they would have been discounted from the people who were actually there! Not only that, but the amount of detail that the authors of the Gospels wrote with is too unbelievably detailed and time stamped to produce a fictitious story.

This is not an exhaustive argument by any stretch of the word, but the logical evidence for me is impossible to ignore.

I'll put it plainly, there is no reason we should be talking about Jesus' death, burial, and resurrection 2000 years after it happened, unless it actually happened. There is no way this story would have survived 2000 years of history because there is no reason the story would have survived the first ten years if it were not true. And, oh by the way, let's not forget to mention that our calendars revolve around the birth of Jesus.

This is all good evidence, but this is not the main reason I believe in the story of Jesus. The main reason I believe in the story of Jesus is by how Jesus' closest followers reacted to his death, and how they reacted after his resurrection.

The Main Event

When I read the story of Jesus' disciples, I love how human they appear to be. Jesus being fully God and fully man was also a human. But I feel like I relate strongly with the disciples who followed Jesus.

Jesus dies, and the disciples run and hide. They are freaking out! Their leader, friend, and teacher was just brutally murdered and then they go out and hide because they are afraid for their lives.

This is the main event for me. What happened after the death of Jesus was these same men who went and hid, were found preaching the Gospel to anyone who would listen wherever they went. Most of these same men who were afraid for their own lives, ended up giving their own lives not proclaiming something they heard, or even something they believed in, but rather proclaiming something they saw! They saw their friend who was certifiably dead, alive. Not only that, but they had breakfast on the beach with him!

Thus began the greatest event in history, the first ever sharing of the main event, the resurrection of Jesus. Anyone who is wrestling with their faith does not have to wrestle with the Church's stance on their faith, or even wrestle with God upfront. The first thing you have to wrestle with is what do you do with the person of Jesus?

Connecting the dots

Jesus was the most polarizing person to ever walk the earth. Even to this day, he still makes waves. Someone that polarizing who proclaims to be the way, the truth, and the life, is worth your time and breath to explore. He may be the only thing worth your time and breath to explore honestly. But lucky for us, he's accessible to us when we try to explore him. He's accessible to us by the written documentation of many people over a short period of time.

I promised you this book would be worth finishing. I believe, as we sit here connecting all of the dots, we can sum it all up this way. The cross took away Jesus' breath. Jesus' death took away your sins. And Jesus' resurrection took away your excuses.

I want you to take something that seems infinite, like seconds you have left in your life, and break them down to something finite, the amount of breath you hold in your lungs. From there, I want you to ask one very important question that I pray allows you to make wiser decisions and experience joy in a way that I have found through Jesus. That question is this: how am I spending the breath God breathed into me?

I believe if you do this, even as an atheist. You can put quotation marks around the word, God, if that helps you. Because after all, you still gotta breathe, right? I believe if you wrestle with this question, you'll make wiser decisions, and have fewer regrets. And when you're on your deathbed, because make no mistake, no matter how much money you make or what you own or how prestigious you are or where you live or what you drive, we all end up on our deathbed. I pray that isn't the time you start getting serious about this Jesus person.

I believe in Jesus. I believe in you.

Time is ticking. Best to get to breathing.

ABOUT THE AUTHOR

Brenton J Ferris is a husband, father, leader, pastor, and writer from Bay City, Michigan. He loves a lot of things, but his wife and his children are at the top of that list. He enjoys a good sense of humor, running, hiking, camping, and rock climbing. He is a marathon runner, enjoys challenges, and engages in his local church as a leader and gifted communicator. His passion is that everyone, everywhere, would engage with the Gospel of Jesus Christ, no matter what they were raised believing.